EMOTIONAL INTELLIGENCE AND ACADEMIC STRESS OF HIGHER SECONDARY STUDENTS

EMOTIONAL INTELLIGENCE AND ACADEMIC STRESS OF HIGHER SECONDARY STUDENTS

By

Dr. Pasupuleti Papa Rao

M.A., M.Sc., M.Ed., M.Phill., APSET., Ph.D

Kandukur (Andhra Pradesh)

DPH

DISCOVERY

PUBLISHING HOUSE

Published by:

DISCOVERY PUBLISHING HOUSE
4383/4B, Ansari Road, Darya Ganj
New Delhi-110 002 (India)
Phone : +91-11-23279245; 23253475; 43596065
Mobile : +91 9811179893 / +91 9871656464
E-mail : discoverybooksindia@gmail.com
orderdphbooks@gmail.com
namitwasan9@gmail.com
web : www.discoverypublishinggroup.com

Emotional Intelligence and Academic Stress of Higher Secondary Students
Author: **Dr. Pasupuleti Papa Rao**

International Standard Book Number: **978-93-6224-781-0** (Hardback)

Printed at:
Infinity Imaging Systems
Delhi (INDIA)

Acknowledgements

I always thank and praise the almighty God, for giving me wisdom without measure, to do my tasks and continue my higher education, whose power make the body and mind sound as well as strong enough and confident to achieve my goals.

I would like to thank all those who were a part of the current that carried me along through the journey of my Doctoral program. There were many, but as with most, I have those special few who went above and beyond the call of the duty in helping me complete the task in time.

First and the foremost is my teacher and research guide **Dr. A. Amruthavalli Devi,** Assistant Professor in Education, University PG Centre, Ongole Camps, Acharya Nagarjuna University, Guntur who gave me strong intellectual direction to think rationally and view things critically, and her guidance was exceptionally balanced with inspiration and encouragement which constantly helped me to complete the work with assurance and confidence. I am blessed with her endurance and persistence.

I am very much thankful to **Dr. Brahmaji Rao**, Head, Department of education, Acharya Nagarjuna University, Guntur for support given to me during the course.

I am very much thankful to **Smt. S. Srilakshmi**, for support given to me during the course.

I express my sincere gratitude to my parents **Sri P. Srinivasa Rao Garu & Smt. P. Ramanamma Garu** for their blessings.

I am grateful to my friends **Dr. Nalamotu Venkateswarlu & Tanikonda Hari Babu** for their valuable support and encourage extended to me throughout my research work.

I express my sincere gratitude to my beloved wife **Smt. P.V. Sivaranjani** for her valuable support and encourage extended to me throughout my research work.

I sincerely thanks to all the Principals of the college who have very kindly given me the time to conduct the test, without whose support this book may not have been completed.

–Pasupuleti Papa Rao

Contents

CHAPTER 1

Introduction

INTRODUCTION

Education is to cater to the holistic development of the students in the pursuit of their goals and teachers in colleges play a significant role. Besides the stress on academic excellence, they have to take care of the student's affective (emotional) dimension. This calls upon the teacher to be first and foremost to draw out the students emotional intelligence. Students unrest, rates of teen suicides, pregnancies, drug addiction, broken families are given much importance but sufficient effort is not made in our educational institutions to develop emotional intelligence.

Education plays a pivotal role in modern society. In recent years, societys interest and concern for Academic Achievement, especially among the younger generation has increased. Academic Achievement is a combination of ability and effort. Presumably, ability being equal, those with higher motivation exerts more effort and will achieve higher grades. Academic Achievement has always been one of the most important goals of the educational process. It is also a major goal that is much expected to pursue in all cultures. It is the product variable that gets toned up or bogged down by the positive and negative influence of a host of independent variables.

Emotional intelligence is being able to monitor our own and others feelings and education to discriminate among them and to use this to guide our thinking, emotions and actions (Salovey & Mayer, 1990). The emotionally intelligent person is skilled in four areas: Identifying, using, understanding and regulating emotions (Salovey & Mayer (1993). According to Goleman (1995) emotional intelligence consists of five components: knowing our emotions (self-awareness), managing them, motivating ourselves, recognizing emotions in others (Empathy) and handling relationships.

MEANING OF EMOTIONAL INTELLIGENCE

Psychology and management researchers were interested in studying human emotions long before the construct of Emotional Intelligence was proposed. Salovey and Mayer (1990) were among the earliest to suggest the name "Emotional intelligence" to refer to the ability of a person to deal with his or her emotions. They defined Emotional Intelligence as "the subset of social intelligence that involves the ability to monitor one's own and others feelings and emotions to discriminate among them and to use this information to guide ones thinking and actions". Despite this early definition of Emotional Intelligence, there has been confusion regarding the exact meaning and domain of this construct. During the early stage of the development of the Emotional Intelligence construct, deferent researchers used slightly deferent definitions of Emotional Intelligence which has led to some variations in the domain of the construct.

Appraisal and expression of emotion in oneself: This is related to an individuals ability to understand his/her deep emotions and to be able to express emotions naturally. People who have good ability in this area will sense and acknowledge their emotions better than most people.

Appraisal and recognition of emotion in others: This is related to an individuals ability to perceive and understand the emotions of the people around them. People who rate highly in this ability will be very sensitive to the emotions of others as well as able to predict others emotional responses.

Regulation of emotion in oneself: This relates to the ability of a person to regulate his/her emotions enabling a more rapid recovery from psychological distress. A person with high ability in this area would be able to return quickly to normal psychological states after recognizing or being upset. Such a person would be less likely to lose his/her temper.

Use of emotion to facilitate performance: This is related to the ability of a person to make use of his (or) her emotions by directing them towards constructive activities and personal performance. A person who is highly capable in this dimension would be able to encourage him-or herself to do better continuously. He or she would also be able to direct his or her emotions in positive and productive directions.

CONCEPT OF EMOTIONAL INTELLIGENCE

Intelligence in Homosephians had been conceptualized in various forms like it comprise of two factors, General (G) and Specific (S) (Spearman 1923) or it is consisting of multifactors (Gardner 1983) or it is a global capacities (Wechsler 1944). However enormous researches have been endeavored to know its true nature and recent researches, have been opined that intelligence of a person is a composite organization of abilities to learn, to grasp bread and subtle facts, especially abstract facts with alertness and accuracy to exercise mental control and to display flexibility and integrity in the solution of problems. In course of studying the true nature of inter relation between emotion and intelligence or reasoning for the first-time, both merged into a single construct named as emotional intelligence by Salovey and Mayer (1990) and was defined to include a group of mental abilities viz, appraisal and expression of emotion, regulating and utilization of emotion. To be more broader other researchers like Goleman (1995) and Bar-on (1997) included some other human characteristics to define emotional intelligence like self control, zeal and persistence, the ability to motivate oneself and an array of non-cognitive capabilities, competencies that influence ones ability to succeed in coping with environmental demands and pressures.

Studies are abundance which establish that general intelligence measured as I.Q. and emotional intelligence of a person are found to be equal or the same (Singh, 2001) however it is evident that presence of high emotional intelligence may ensure more success and happiness in ones life as well as in professional life than having only high intelligence or I.Q. For a student as well as for a worker, success can be found out not only by this high intelligence quotient rather than he needs a high or moderate level of emotional intelligence to be well adjusted in a highly competitive world.

Until the establishment of the concept of Mayer, Salovey and Caruso (2000) that intelligence (reasoning) and emotions can work hand in the form of emotional intelligence (Strongman 1965; young 1986). However not only intelligence, other correlated of emotional intelligence have been tried to be endeavored in empirical studies like intelligence (I.Q) Interpersonal relations, success in personal and work life, managing occupational stress and many more positive behavior patterns. It is noticed that potentialities like creativity of a person has yet to be studied in the context of emotional intelligence particularly among the adolescents.

The epidemiological statistics of psychosomatic problems is increasing day by day and is a major challenge to medical and psychological researcher. An individual feel more powerful and successful than he has been ever felt. IQ and EQ are not opposing competencies but rather separate ones. Emotional Intelligence adds for more of the qualities that make us more human. Emotional Intelligence helps the people to mange better their feelings of anger, anxiety, depression and loneliness and is a form of disease prevention. Childhood and adolescence are critical periods for building essential emotional Intelligence. E.L Thorndike, an eminent psychologist proposed in a Harper's Magazine articles that one aspect of emotional intelligence, social intelligence -the ability to understand others and act wisely in human relations. Emotional intelligence is a Meta ability which involves in handling raw intellect. Emotional quotient as a measure of a person's ability to identify and use emotions effectively is a new concept. Emotional disturbance is a major symptom in Neuroses and Psychosis. In a country like India, with rich traditional beliefs and culture, most of the people are externals. They view their behavior as influenced by events that are completely out of their control due to such factors as chance, powerful figures in authority and fate. Internal and external locus of control is one of the potential determinates of behavior (Rotter, 1972). Yale psychologist peter Salovey, invented the concept of Emotional intelligence (EI) together with university of New Hampshire psychologist John Mayer, in 1990. "Motivating oneself despite persistent setback", and "staying hopeful". Salovey talks about 5 abilities when he defines Emotional Intelligence. They are know ones emotions, managing emotions, motivating one, recognizing emotions drawn from family. It converts disempowering signals of guilt, anxiety, depression they bring into states of compassion, interest and internal power. Skill in emotional regulation makes (Bar-one 1997) maintained that emotional intelligence is an arrange of non-cognitive capabilities, competencies, and skills that influence ones ability to succeed in coping with environmental demands and pressures. He includes five major areas of skills: Interpersonal skills, interpersonal skills, adaptability skills positive impression skills, adaptability skills and positive impression skills. The ability model of emotional intelligence focuses on the interplay of emotional and intelligence as traditionally defined. Where as the mixed models describe a kind of compound conception of intelligence that includes mental abilities. The mental ability models focuses on emotions themselves and their interactions with thought (Mayer & Salovey, 1997; Salovey & Mayer, 1997) where as mixed models treat mental abilities and a variety of other characteristics such as motivation, state of consciousness and social activity as a single entity (Bar-on, 1997; Goleman. 1995).

According to mixed model, emotional - social intelligence is a cross-section of interrelated emotional and social competencies, skills and facilitators that determine how effectively we understand and express ourselves, understand others and related with them, and cope with daily demands. This is based first and foremost on ones intrapersonal ability to be aware of ones self, to understand ones strengths and weakness, and to express ones feelings and thoughts non-destructively. On the interpersonal level, being emotionally and social intelligence encompasses the ability to be aware of others emotions, feelings and needs to establish and maintain cooperative, constructive, mutually satisfying relationships. Ultimately, being emotionally and socially intelligence means to effectively manage personal, social and environmental change by realistically, flexibly coping with the immediate situation, solving problems and making decisions.

NATURE OF EMOTIONAL INTELLIGENCE

Emotional Intelligence has its roots in the concept of social intelligence first identified by Thorndike in 1920. Thorndike (1920) defined social intelligence as "the ability to understand and manage men and women, boys and girls – to act wisely in human relations". Gardner (1993) included interpersonal and intrapersonal intelligence in his theory of multiple intelligence. According to Gardner, social intelligence, one among seven intelligence domains comprises an individuals interpersonal and intrapersonal intelligences. Intrapersonal intelligence relates to ones ability to deal with one self and to "symbolize complex and highly differentiated sets of feelings" within the self. Interpersonal intelligence relates to ones ability to deal with others and to "notice and make destinations among other individuals and in particular among their moods, temperaments, motivations and intentions". Emotional Intelligence can be viewed as a combination of the intrapersonal and interpersonal intelligence of an individual.

Given its roots in social intelligence, Mayer et al. (2000) argued that the conceptual back ground of Emotional Intelligence set traditional standards for intelligence measures. They highlighted three criteria that qualify Emotional Intelligence as a fact of intelligence. These are conceptual, correlation, and developmental criteria. The conceptual criterion required that Emotional Intelligence reflect mental abilities instead of preferred ways of behaving. Intelligence refers to "the ability of a person". Gardner (1993) defined intelligence as "the ability to solve problems or to fashion products that are valued in one or more cultural or community settings". To full fill the conceptual criterion and label Emotional Intelligence as an intelligence fact, one must provide evidence that Emotional Intelligence is not a personality trait or a preferred way of behaving but is itself a set of abilities. It is argued conceptually that Emotional Intelligence is defined as a set of abilities on the basis of its theoretical definition. Emotional Intelligence consists of a set of abilities that a person used to understand, regulate and make use of his or her emotions. Emotional understanding, regulation and utilization reflect the capability of a person to manage his/her emotions. Some people have higher competence to do so and some have less competence. As a particular type of competence, Emotional Intelligence is different from personality traits that reflect tendencies to think, feel and behave in certain ways. There is also empirical evidence that EI abilities are distinct from personality traits. When developing the multifactor emotional intelligence scale, Mayer and Salovey (1997) provided some preliminary data to show that EI was different from personality traits.

Mayer et al., (2000) second criterion is the correlation criterion. If Emotional Intelligence is an intelligence facet, it should represent a set of correlated abilities that are similar but distinct from, mental abilities. In other words, if Emotional Intelligence is an intelligence facet it should correlate with other intelligence facets such as GMAS. These correlations cannot be too high nor can they be too low. Both Mayer et al. and Wong & low (2002) showed empirically that the dimensions of Emotional Intelligence were moderately correlated among themselves but only mildly correlated with general mental abilities. Therefore some empirical evidence that Emotional Intelligence meets the correlated criterion of an intelligence facet.

Mayer et al (2000) third argument is that Emotional Intelligence could be conceptualized as intelligence should be developmental in nature. For example the verbal ability of a person should increase as one becomes more mature. Wong, Wong, and law (2002) found that Emotional Intelligence is positively correlated with age among incumbents of six different types of jobs. Mayer et al. also showed with a series of studies, that Emotional Intelligence increased with age and experience that qualifies it as ability rather than a personality trait.

DOMAINS OF EMOTIONAL INTELLIGENCE

Emotional intelligence is essential premise of E.Q: to be successful requires the effective awareness, control and management of ones own emotions, and those of other people. EQ embraces two aspects of intelligence.

1. Understanding ones self, goals, intentions responses, behaviour and skills.
2. Understanding others and their feelings.

Goleman identified the five domains of EQ as:

- Knowing ones own emotions.
- Managing own emotions.
- Motivating oneself.
- Recognizing and understanding other people s emotions.
- Managing relationships, i.e., managing the emotions of others.

1. Self-awareness

The awareness of ones feeling and the ability to recognize and the ability to manage these feelings in a way which one feels that one can control. This factor includes a degree of self-belief in ones ability to manage ones emotions and to control them in a work environment.

2. Emotional resilience

The ability to perform consistently in a range of situations under pressure and to adapt behaviour appropriately. The ability to balance the needs of the situation and task with the needs and concerns of the individuals involved. The ability to retain focus on a course of action or need for results in the face of personal challenge or criticism.

3. Motivation

The drive and energy to active clear results and make on impact and also to balance short and long term goals with an ability to pursue demanding goals in the face of rejection or questioning.

4. Interpersonal sensitivity

The ability to be aware of and take account of the needs and perceptions of others are in arriving at decisions and proposing solutions to problems and challenges. The ability to build from this awareness and achieve the commitment of others to decisions and action ideas. The willing to keep open ones thoughts on possible solutions to problems, to actively listen to and reflect on the reactions and inputs from others.

5. Influence

The ability to persuade others to change a view point based on the understanding of their position and the recognition of the need to listen to this perspective and provide a rationale for change.

6. Intuitiveness

The ability to arrive at clear decisions and drive their implementation when presented with incomplete or ambiguous information using both rational and emotional or intuitive perceptions of key issues and implication.

7. Conscientiousness

The ability to display clear commitment to action in the face of challenge and to match words and deeds in encouraging others to support the choose direction. The personal commitment to pursing on ethical solution to a difficult issue or problem.

Components of Emotional Intelligence:

1. Perception, appraisal and expression of emotions.
2. Emotional facilitation of thinking.
3. Understanding and analyzing emotions-employing emotional knowledge.
4. Relative regulations of emotions to promote emotional and intellectual growth.

Enhancing Emotional Intelligence

One can increase Intelligence Quotient by immersing himself in books. To improve Emotional Quotient one need the help of other people like psychologist, counselors, Educational psychologist, psychiatrist and social worker. Sometimes people that we dislike intensely will be our greatest helpers individual counseling and group therapy can be places to explore stock emotions.

Emotional Quotient in reading and memorize understanding and cognitive development, pupil service and management stimulus motivation cases change, reduces stress improves communication and enhances decision making.

Emotional Quotient positively impacts the ability to sustain both mental and physical health.

- Emotional Quotient empowers romantic relationship enabling to attract others.
- Emotional Quotient permits to raise unbidden high Emotional Quotient and create loving families.
- Because of high Emotional Quotient one can identify, express ones feelings.
- Emotional Quotient allows to address fears using reason rather than avoiding them or allowing them to paralyze you.
- Because of high Emotional Quotient one can empathize with others feelings, acknowledge them and seek to help soothe them.
- Today emotional problems are on the rise all over the world. Moreover, one cannot make good decision without being aware of own feelings and emotions. Emotions are the common bond which can be a potential unit at all places. It is heartening to note that students, parents, teachers, managers and professionals can raise the level of emotional intelligence.

SIGNIFICANCE OF EMOTIONAL INTELLIGENCE

Emotional intelligence has been applied in various settings. Five main components concerning the medical field describe Emotional intelligence. Intrapersonal components include emotional self-awareness, assertiveness, self-regard, self-actualization, and independence. Similarly, interpersonal components include empathy, social responsibility and interpersonal relationships. In addition, adaptability is highlighted by problem solving, reality testing and flexibility and stress management can be described by stress tolerance and impulse control and general mood is shown through happiness and optimism. These components are essential for medical leadership and involve concrete results in medical education, professional relationships, development and patients care.

Emotional intelligence offers a teaching framework that allows learning from collaborative relationships in order to increase professional development and leadership. Emotional learning and maturation are paramount to both. Emotional intelligence is a quality that improves and optimizes by personal reflection, practice and supervision. The Emotional intelligence physician consolidates a supportive work climate, encouraging high-efficiency in which other health professionals feel energized to perform better in a mutual confidence ambiance.

Moreover relationships between colleagues, Emotional intelligence training could lead to better work/life balance and doctor-patient relations. Emotional intelligence physician builds resilience and copes with stressful periods as well as experiences better physical and psychological health. Hence physicians care for themselves through self-awareness and reflection which appears to be one of the most important things to provide good care to others. Being more sensitive to their own and their patients feelings and emotions, Emotional intelligence physicians use supportive behavior and provide psychological benefit.

Leaders challenge remains in becoming familiar with a powerful combination made of knowledge and relation management. Emotional intelligence can be learned, developed and reinforced with life experience. Emotional intelligence is accessible if we decide to consider it to be a resource and not a sentimental weakness only if we support its emergence in our daily lifestyle.

Goleman (1995) observations with respect to emotional intelligence:

The dynamic interrelation of the cortex and the limbic systems are important. The cortex is considered as the seat of rationality while the limbic system is the part of the brain where the emotions are processed. The concept of EI is explained to mean the moderation of primitive emotional impulses by the rational mind and suggests that the emotional intelligence can be learnt with practice.

- IQ plays only 20% to the success of an individual while 80% success is based on ones EI. He observes that many high IQ scoring students have failed in their practical lives, while many average people with higher EI have got phenomenal success.
- A reflexive mode of experience (self-awareness or self-observation) is deemed to be important. Emotional competencies like emotional self-control are built on the fundamental competency self-awareness.
- We have two minds – one an emotional mind that feels and other, a rational mind that thinks. Emotions are fed in to the operations of the rational mind and the rational mind refines the inputs of emotions. Thus there is a balance between emotional and rational minds.

- One may be more attuned to emotional mind's special symbols such as metaphors, similes, poetry, songs and fables. If so then one should try his success in these fields instead of following predictions made by the IQ tests. Emotional adjustments make a person more gifted than others.
- We have two brains – emotional brain and rational (thinking). Emotional brain is involved in reasons as is the thinking brain. Also, the thinking brain plays a role in executing our emotions.
- Emotional disorders need pharmacological help. However, there are certain disorders like manic-depression where the patient never feels any need for medication. Severe emotional disorders can hamper ones success if not handled properly.
- Depression, anger and the like are negative emotions. When one is depressed, s/he needs to focus his/her attention to some upbeat activity and avoid tragic movies, novels and stories which will drag his/her mood further down. One should experience (face) anger by assuming that anger belongs to some other person. Empathy is considered as a balm for anger.
- Enthusiasm and persistence are important emotional traits. Most of the Asian students show better record of success than their white counterparts, not for their IQ level but persistence to improve their weaknesses.
- Self-efficacy, the belief that one has mastery over the events of ones life, is the underlying quality behind optimism and hope.
- Women are more empathetic than men. Empathy helps in romantic life and demonstrates an appreciation of emotions as an instrument of knowledge.
- Emotions play an important role in married life. The amount of emotions expressed by each sex during the different times of their lives is focused. Children might have good friends from the opposite sexes in their early lives but slowly lose their interest until they achieve teenage years.
- Generally girls can express their emotions better than boys. The reason for this lies in the fact that girls learn languages more quickly than boys do.
- Men are reluctant to talk with their wives about their relationship and also men may have a rosier view than their wives, of just about everything in relationship. Wives, in general, are more vocal about their complaints than their husbands, particularly among unhappy couples.

- Stars in the Emotional Intelligence tests were the people who used to get their work finished in stipulated time. EI was found to be one of the main characteristics of successful people. People with average or below average scorers in the emotional intelligence test were those who start many tasks at a time and leave most of them unfinished. It is one of the reasons behind most of the unsuccessful people.
- Health and emotions are inter-related. Chemical messengers that operate most extensively in both brain and immune system are those that are most dense in neural areas that regulate emotion.
- People who experience chronic anxiety, long periods of sadness and pessimism, unremitting tension or incessant hostility, relentless cynicism or suspiciousness, face double the risk of disease including asthma, arthritis, headaches, peptic ulcers, and heart disease.
- Children who are often subjected to beating by their parents react in the same way in distress. They lose empathy if they have to face such situations frequently.
- When a person faces trauma, s/he may end up in biological crisis. But the problem becomes severe when an individual is placed in an uncontrollable stress.
- Temperament is not Destiny. People having strong right frontal activity are prone to be moody, suspicious of the world and worried about small problems. People with strong left frontal activity are lower in depression, more confident and rewardingly engaged in life.
- Some people are unable to differentiate between being scared and angry. They feel more hunger in depressing situations and eat more only to gain weight. People with few friends or with extreme tendencies for loneliness are at great risk of diseases and early death.
- EI is a capacity that profoundly affects all other abilities, either facilitating or interfering with them. Training programmes can help children to be assertive and to articulate their feelings in situations involving conflict with others

MEANING AND NATURE OF ACADEMIC STRESS

The word stress is derived from the Latin word "stringi", which means "to be drawn tight". Stress can be defined as any factor that threatens the health of the body or has an adverse effect on its functioning such as injury, disease, or worry. According to Randy and David (2008) "Stress is the subjective feeling produced by events that are uncontrollable or threatening." Constant stress brings about changes in the balance of hormones in the body which may lead to the situation or thought that makes us feel frustrated, angry, nervous, or anxious.

Academic Stress is an important factor accounting for variation in academic achievement. It also contributes to major mental health hazards, problems both physical and mental stress related diseases. Stress makes a significant contribution to the prediction of subsequent school performance and act as a negative predictor of academic performance in school children.

Academic stress refers to the pressure to perform well in final school examinations and competitive college entrance examinations that is experienced by students. For some students, the experience of academic stress leads to a sense of distress which is generally manifested in a variety of psychological and behavioral problems. The experience of academic stress and adolescent distress has been identified and explored by many researchers.

Academic stress and adolescent distress has not been explored in great detail in India. It is important to note that this issue is one that affects a small proportion of Indian youth, those who are fortunate enough to attend and graduate from high school. Mental health professionals in India have identified academic pressure as an acute stress factor that leads to mental distress and in extreme cases to suicide. Around examination time and when examination results are announced, when academic stress is very high, suicide hotlines in many cities across the country are swamped with calls.

Youth suicide is only the tip of the iceberg which masks the generalized anxiety and depression experienced by many high school students. Studies conducted in Korea and Japan have found that students who experience academic stress express their distress in a variety of ways in terms of depression, anxiety, and somatic symptoms (Lee and Larson, 1996; Schoolland, 1990). Research studies in India have not explored these particular forms of distress with respect to academic stress. Hence the extent and prevalence of the problem is unknown. Furthermore, there have been no studies conducted in India or elsewhere that explore the issue from the perspective of the student and the experience of academic stress and adolescent distress remains relatively unexplored.

Research suggests that there are many sources of academic stress. Students may feel stressed and as a result distressed by their own high academic expectations. In addition to their personal experiences of stress and distress, studies identify many other sources of academic stress including parents, teachers, school administrators, and larger societal origins. A large body of research suggests that parents have a particularly strong influence on their childs education in a variety of ways. Studies conducted with western samples have found that parents may have high expectations for their childs future, hold positive beliefs about their childs abilities and involve themselves in their child s education.

Studies conducted with East Asian immigrant families have identified other ways in which parents may be involved in their childs education. For instance, researchers have found that many parents make financial and social adjustments to their lifestyle in order to advance their childs academic and professional outcomes or create an environment that promotes academic achievement (Kim, 1993; Schneider & Lee, 1990). While Indian parents are known to be deeply involved in their children s education (Larson, Verma and Dworkin, 2000), at present, little is known about the role of parents in the student experience of academic stress and adolescent distress.

Research studies suggest that academic stress can have serious consequences for students. Very little is known about the topic in India which suggests that it requires urgent investigation. This is a particularly interesting moment in Indian history in which to explore the issue because there has been significant social change in India since the early 1990s. According to Inkeles (1998), there are four forces that lead to societal change. These forces can be technological changes in the structure of the economy, ecological which are changes in the way people use space; legal, which are changes in governance and institutions and cultural, which are changes in norms and values. These changes are slowly altering the traditional social hierarchy and creating new educational and professional opportunities for youth.

CAUSES OF ACADEMIC STRESS

Academic pressure is a significant source of stress for many of the students (Hashim, 2003; Olpin, 1997; Tyrrell, 1992). Identified sources of academic-related stress have included fear of falling behind with coursework, finding the motivation to study, time pressures, financial worries, and concern about academic ability (Tyrrell, 1992). Additionally, students report stress over struggling to meet academic standards, time management worries, and concerns over grades (Olpin, 1997). These sources may exist easily throughout the span of college students. If prevention efforts are to be developed to assist students in dealing with and avoiding academic-related stress, a greater understanding of the relationship among school students use of coping strategies, social support, experiences of being parented and academic-related stress needs to be gained. Causes of stress on students include both positive and negative.

Academics: Alphabetically first among the causes of stress on students is academic pressure. Simply tackling more difficult assignments can demand stress management techniques. It might be wise for teachers to introduce students to this stress with an assignment such as a "Causes of Stress on Students Essay". Requiring students to interview older students and educators as well as research in Internet on the subject could help them prepare for the stresses of academic challenges.

Dating: Student life throughout high school and college is filled with thinking about dating, dating, trying to date, failing to date and being dumped. The mating game is filled with estruses, but it also involves distress and is among the greatest causes of stress on students.

Environment: The school environment itself can be a cause of stress on students. Students moving into secondary education find it challenging to constantly move around to classes. Those matriculating to tertiary education are challenged with leaving home and establishing a new life in new setting. Both can cause stress on students.

Extra Co-curricular: Colleges pressure high school students to engage in extracurricular activities such as choirs, clubs, sports, band, or volunteer work. The presence of these on a student application can go far toward acceptance. Hence college extracurricular activities still cause stress on students, once their presence on a job application is also an asset.

Peers: Like dating, peer relationships can provide estruses or distress. As peers apply pressure in regard to dress, behavior, choice of friends and many other areas of life pressure can become a huge presence of stress on students.

Parental Pressure: Students experience stress from parental pressures. Parents want their children to succeed in school. They want to see good grades but they also want to see success in lifes other areas. In their attempts to guide their children, parents can become one of the major causes of stress on students. It is wise for parents and others who work with students to take time to recognize the stresses students face, if they provide stress management techniques, they will do much to relieve and encourage their students.

SYMPTOMS OF ACADEMIC STRESS

Some of the important symptoms that indicate stress include: psychosomatic complaints like head-ache, migration and ulcer etc.

1. Increased susceptibility to illness.
2. Increased irritability, low frustration tolerance, sadness, panic and anger.
3. Restlessness, depression, inability to concentrate.
4. Lack of self-esteem, sense of despair, etc.

The world is becoming more and more competitive. Quality of performance has become the key factor for personal progress. Parents desire that their children climb the ladder of performance to a high level as possible. This desire for high level of achievement put a lot of pressure on students, teachers and in the educational system itself.

Interest in Stress and its effects on human beings has received considerable attention during the past three decades. Hans Selye (1981) was the pioneer in the twentieth century who gave impetus to the interest of psychologists to pay attention to the role of stress on physical wellbeing. His research is based on the works of Claude Bernard (1859) and Walter Cannon (1929). Bernard demonstrated the value of stability of internal environment and insisted on its maintenance at all cost. Walter Cannon said that fight and flight is an essential mechanism for survival. Thus scientific study of stress has become an integral part of Psychobiological Sciences.

The most important fact concerning the term stress is its persistence, wide spread usage in Biology and Psychology. In todays life, Stress has become so significant in everybodys life and its has become pervasive and major concern for Scientists in various fields i.e. Medicine, Psychology, Sociology, Neurobiology, Environmental science etc. Thus research in the above said fields is directly or indirectly concerned with the question of understanding the antecedent and consequences of stress and its management in such a way that quality of life of people is improved. A problem of such magnitude requires having proper understanding of the concept of stress and its related phenomena so that we may handle our own life as well as those of others.

Despite the fact that education is universally given a high priority, the academic institutions today do not show a motivating atmosphere. Students are often subjected to various stress related tests, examinations, excessive homework, teachers biased attitude, peer group pressure etc. The major challenges of children are: Poor retention and recall, lack of appreciation from their parents, school environment, personal anxieties, fear of teachers, examination phobia, perpetual insecurity, conflicting expectations from the parents and the society, the growing competition, fear of failure or success etc.

Some amount of academic stress is essential in mobilizing the potentialities of the individuals to work more efficiently. But increased amount for a prolonged period will have deleterious effects on the physical and mental health and academic achievement of the students. The common symptoms include: diminished pleasure in learning, addiction to drugs, alcohol, smoking, irritability, fatigue, depression, insomnia, and physical problems ranging from migraine and back pains to ulcers. A general survey of related literature shows adaptation of various resources or strategies by students in an effort to cope with the academic stress at work. Some of them may be adequate and others inadequate causing further stress and pushing the student into a vicious circle of academic stress and maladaptive behavior.

The management through principal plays a very important role in student burnout and stress both as a major source of support and the main source of support and the main source of stress. Students often cite stress as a reason for poor performance. These negative relations may lead to stress, induced illness behavior in students.

NEED AND SIGNIFICANCE OF THE STUDY

In today's highly competitive world, students face various academic problems including exam stress, disinterest in attending classes and inability to understand the subject. Academic stress is the feeling of anxiety or apprehension over one's performance in the academic activities. It can lead to students being unable to perform to the best of their abilities in examinations. At school/college there is a range of academic pressure feel derived from a need for perfection, worry over grades, parental pressure, competition, sports, or a tough class load.

In 2019, the Ministry of Human Resource Development released a Draft New Education Policy 2019, which was followed by a number of public consultations. The Draft NEP discusses reducing curriculum content to enhance essential learning, critical thinking and more holistic 8 experiential, discussion-based and analysis-based learning. It also talks about a revision of the curriculum and pedagogical structure from a 10+2 system to a 5+3+3+4 system design in an effort to optimize learning for students based on cognitive development of children.

The nervous breakdowns, panic attacks, burnouts, and depression are also apparent in many younger students. The same situation is not always stressful for all people and all people do not undergo the same feelings or off-putting thoughts when stressed. Students were considered to be the future pillars who take the responsibilities to take our country to the next phase they should be in better way.

Students with high emotional quotient know and manage their own emotional life well and understand and deal effectively with the feelings of others. They are skillful in relationships. Intermediate course as an area of interdisciplinary knowledge is not merely an application of new core disciplines, but a praxis of a content where theories and practical wisdom are generated continuously. In working towards holistic approach to education, the importance of an emotionally supportive environment in the classroom is created by a teacher. Emotionally healthy behavior is reflected in characteristic ways of thinking, identifying, managing and expressing feelings and choosing effective behaviours. Emotional experience and expression are unique to each teacher and student. To know this, the investigator decided to analysis the emotional intelligence and academic stress among intermediate students.

STATEMENT OF THE PROBLEM

An attempt is made in the present investigation to study the impact of Emotional intelligence and Academic Stress among Intermediate Students. In addition the impact of gender, locality, Management, Medium, Mother's Education, Father's Education, Mother's Occupation, Father's Occupation, Family Income, Birth Order, Size of the family and Type of the family on the variables such as Emotional Intelligence and Academic Stress were also attempted.

The present study is stated as "A study on Emotional Intelligence and Academic Stress among Intermediate Students".

OPERATIONAL DEFINITIONS OF KEY TERMS:

(i) Emotional Intelligence

*Emotional intelligence is the ability to possess emotional information particularly as it involves the perception, assimilation, understanding and management of emoti.*ons

–Mayers Salovey and David Caruso (2000)

"Emotional intelligence is a innate potential depend on the ability to feel emotions includes ability to remember feelings"

–Steve Hein (2005)

In the present investigation an attempt is made to study the influence of various dependent variables on emotional intelligence of intermediate students.

(ii) Academic Stress

Academic stress is over struggling to meet academic standards, time management worries, and concerns over grades

–(Olpin, 1997)

Academic pressure is a significant source of stress for much school/college students.

–(Hashim, 2003)

In the present investigation an influence of various dependent variables on academic stress of intermediate students have been studied.

OBJECTIVES OF THE STUDY

Keeping in view of need of the study the following objectives are formulated for the present investigation.

1. To assess the level of emotional intelligence and academic stress among intermediate students.

2. To study the influence of main effect and interaction effect of gender, management and locality on emotional intelligence and academic stress among intermediate students.
3. To find weather there is any significant influence of the following Socio-demographic variables on Emotional Intelligence and Academic Stress of Intermediate Students.
    (a) Gender
    (b) Management
    (c) Locality
    (d) Nature of Course
    (e) Medium
    (f) Caste
    (g) Mother's Education
    (h) Father's Education
    (i) Mother's Occupation
    (j) Father's Occupation
    (k) Annual Income of the Family
    (l) Size of the Family
    (m) Type of the Family
4. To find weather there is any significant relationship between emotional intelligence and academic stress of intermediate students.
5. To find the levels of Emotional Intelligence and Academic Stress of Intermediate students with reference to the main variables gender, locality and type of management.

HYPOTHESES OF THE STUDY

Based on the above objectives the following null hypotheses are formulated for the present study.

1. There would be no significant influence of the main effects of gender, management and locality on emotional intelligence and academic stress of intermediate students.
2. There would be no significant impact of interaction effect of gender, management and locality on emotional intelligence and academic stress of intermediate students.
3. There would be no significant influence of Gender on Emotional Intelligence and Academic Stress of Intermediate Students.
4. There would be no significant influence of Management on Emotional Intelligence and Academic Stress of Intermediate Students.

5. There would be no significant influence of Locality on Emotional Intelligence and Academic Stress of Intermediate Students.
6. There would be no significant influence of Nature of Course on Emotional Intelligence and Academic Stress of Intermediate Students.
7. There would be no significant influence of Medium on Emotional Intelligence and Academic Stress of Intermediate Students.
8. There would be no significant influence of Type of residence on Emotional Intelligence and Academic Stress of Intermediate Students.
9. There would be no significant influence of Caste on Emotional Intelligence and Academic Stress of Intermediate Students.
10. There would be no significant influence of Father's Education on Emotional Intelligence and Academic Stress of Intermediate Students.
11. There would be no significant influence of Mother's Education on Emotional Intelligence and Academic Stress of Intermediate Students.
12. There would be no significant influence of Father's Occupation on Emotional Intelligence and Academic Stress of Intermediate Students.
13. There would be no significant influence of Mother's Occupation on Emotional Intelligence and Academic Stress of Intermediate Students.
14. There would be no significant influence of Family Income on Emotional Intelligence and Academic Stress of Intermediate Students.
15. There would be no significant influence of Size of the Family on Emotional Intelligence and Academic Stress of Intermediate Students.
16. There would be no significant influence of Type of the Family on Emotional Intelligence and Academic Stress of Intermediate Students.
17. These would be no significant relationship between Emotional Intelligence and Academic Stress of Intermediate Students.
18. There would be no significant difference in the levels of Emotional Intelligence of Intermediate students with respect to the variables Gender, Locality and Type of management.
19. There would be no significant difference in the levels of Academic Stress of Intermediate students with respect to the variables Gender, Locality and Type of management.

SCOPE OF THE STUDY

The intention of the study is to make a survey of emotional intelligence and academic stress of students studying of intermediate in various colleges located in Guntur, Prakasam and Nellore districts of Andhra Pradesh state. This constituted the population of the study. The study attempted to identify the influence of the dependent variables, Emotional Intelligence and Academic Stress on the independent variables Gender, Management, Locality, Nature of Course, Medium, Caste, Father's Education, Mother's Education,

Father's Occupation, Mother's Occupation, Annual Income of the Family, Size of the Family and Type of the Family.

DELIMITATIONS OF THE STUDY

The following delimitations are observed in this investigation.

1. The study is limited to the students of 2nd year intermediate course only.
2. Due to time limitations only certain variables namely Emotional Intelligence, Academic Stress and socio demographic variables are studied in this investigation.
3. Intermediate Colleges in Gutur, Prakasam and Nellore districts of Andhra Pradesh state.
4. The effect of only a few independent variables on Emotional Intelligence, Academic Stress has been studied.
5. The Emotional Intelligence scores are taken only from intermediate students and this scale was adopted.
6. The Academic Stress scores are taken only from intermediate students and this scale constructed and revised by the investigator.
7. The study is based on survey research, where in the techniques of analyzing the data, are based on the questionnaires only.

ORGANIZATION OF THE REPORT

The study is presented in five chapters.

Chapter-1 deals with Introduction, Need and significance of the study, Statement of the problem, Operational definitions of key terms, objectives, Hypothesis, Scope of the Study, Delimitations of the study and Organisation of the Study.

Chapter-2 contains review of related studies in four classifications.

Chapter-3 describes methodology followed in the conduct of the study. This includes method of study, tools selected and used in the study, sample selected, data collection, statistical techniques employed.

Chapter-4 presents analysis of data collected and results obtained.

Chapter-5 concludes the present study. Includes summary, findings and suggestions.

CHAPTER 2

Review of Related Literature

INTRODUCTION

Researches take advantage of the knowledge which has accumulated in the past, as a result of constant human endeavor. It can never be under taken in the isolation of the work, which has already been done on the problems which are directly or indirectly related to a study proposed by the research, journal, books, dissertations, theses and other sources of information on the problem to be planning of any research study. A careful review of related literature must any well-planned research study.

REVIEW OF RELATED STUDIES ON EMOTIONAL INTELLIGENCE

Gender Vs Emotional Intelligence

Bharadwaj (1997) focused on the need for achievement in relation to adequate expression and control of emotions and sex among handicapped (i.e., congenitally blind and cerebral palsied) and non handicapped children on a sample of six hundred subjects ranging between eight to fourteen years by following a 2×2×3 factorial design. It is discerned that higher need for achievement emerges as a prominent need among handicapped children.

Bharadwaj (1998) explored the prospects of emotional competence associated with early adolescent labourers and non labourers of both sexes on a sample of 600 early adolescents by employing a two group design. The twelve independent studies brought to for that in comparison to female non labourers, female labourers possess greater emotional competence. Male labourers have greater adequate expression and control of emotions than male non labourers whereas ability to function with emotions and encouragement of positive emotions has been found to be greater in both male and female labourers as compared to non labourers of the sexes. The prominence of better emotional competencies among labourers than non labourers posses a great need for reorient our policies with regard to child labour instead of it pseudo eradication endeavors.

Pradhan et al., (1999) examined the concept of EQ competencies and leadership effectiveness in middle level managers in India. Their study reported a positive relationship between the two.

Petrides and Adrian Fumham (2000) studied gender differences in measured and self estimated trait emotional intelligence. Results revealed that females scored higher than males on the social skills factor of measured trait emotional intelligence. However, the 15 facets of self estimated emotional intelligence were combined into a single reliable scale and the participants measured trait emotional intelligence scores were held constant, it was demonstrated that males believed they had higher for males that females, most of the correlations between measured and self estimated scores were significant and positive, thereby indicating that people have some insight into their emotional intelligence correlations between measured and self estimated scores were generally higher for males that females, and a regression analysis indicated that gender was a significant predictor of self estimated emotional intelligence.

Ciarrochi, Chan, and Bajgar (2001) examined the concept of emotional intelligence in adolescents. It was found that emotional intelligence in adolescents was higher for females than males and was positively associated with the skill of identifying emotional expressions, amount of social support, extent of satisfaction with social support and mood management behaviour.

Asha (2003) examined the effect of creativity, intelligence and academic stress on mental health of students. The sample consisted of 126 students (61 male and 65 female) in Calicut city. Descriptive Test of Creativity by Shen Gupta, Mental Abilities Test by Mathew.

Academic Stress Scale by Singh and Mental Health Inventory by Anand Kumar were administered to subjects. Findings suggested that the high creative and high intelligent groups of both male and female students experienced less stress and better mental health than the less creative and less intelligent students both male and female.

Saroj (2003) examined the emotional intelligence among college students and its relationship to their general will being. The sample consisted of 120 college students. Emotional intelligence scale by Schutte and P.F.I measure of general will being by Verma and Verma were employed on post graduate students. Two extreme groups were drawn on the basis of scores on emotional intelligence measure high and low scores on emotional intelligence (male and female separately) were compared regarding their general well being. The male and female students, who scored higher on emotional intelligence scored significantly higher for general well being.

Pathan (2004) conducted a study on emotional intelligence of secondary teachers at D.Ed. College, Navapur, Maharashtra. This study examined the level of emotional intelligence (EI) of secondary school teachers in relation to gender and age. The tool used for the study was a structured questionnaire called, Emotional Intelligence Test, developed by Chadha and Singh (2001). The results indicated that nearly all the teachers under study were under low category of emotional intelligence. There was no significant difference between the emotional intelligence of males and females, and the age was independent of EI.

Rabindra Kumar (2005) probed the relationship between Emotional Intelligence and Personal Effectiveness. It was hypothesized that Emotional Intelligence enhances personal effectiveness. The study was conducted on 50 college students (25 males and 25 females) from various departments of Delhi University. The sample was administered Emotional Intelligence Scale (Cooper and Sawat) and Personal Effectiveness Scale (Udai Pareek, 1989).

Amritha & Kadhirvan (2006) carried out research on "the influence on personality on the emotional intelligence of teachers". The results revealed that gender, age and qualification will influence the emotional intelligence of teachers. It was also noted that thinking, judging dimension of personality here significance positive impact on emotional intelligence.

Patil and Kumar (2006) find out the difference in the emotional intelligence of male and female student teachers of arts and science faculty. Emotional Intelligence Test (EIT) and academic achievement score were used as research tool in the study. Findings revealed that there is no significant difference between emotional intelligence of male and female student teachers of arts and science faculty. There is no significant relationship between the emotional intelligence and academic achievement of student teachers.

The study by Bindu and Immanuel (2006) on Gender differences in Emotional Intelligence investigated the nature and extent of the relationship that exists among two cognitive variables, viz. Intelligence and Creativity, and two non-cognitive variables, viz. Emotional Intelligence and Maladjustment among a sample of young adults (n=90) of Arts (21), Science (11), Humanities (27) and Management (31) departments. The results revealed that the two gender groups differed significantly in the mean scores on the variables and also in their inter-correlations. Maladjustment was identified as the most important predictor of all the other variables, in the case of male sample. Emotional Intelligence played a significant role in determining overall creativity and maladjustment in the female sample. The relationship between Intelligence and creativity was found to be stronger in female group than in the male group.

Suresh (2007) studied the effect of the emotional intelligence as a correlate of mental health of students. The sample consists of 602 male and female, arts and science group students. Mental Health Questionnaire by Anand and Emotional Intelligence by Sharma were used in the study. Results revealed that male and female students differed significantly in their mental health and science and arts student teachers did not differed significantly in their mental health.

Bala, Agarwal and Sarna (2009) studied the gender differences as associated with mental health of students. Major findings of the study were Gender difference exists with reference to various aspects of mental health. Boys had greater emotional stability, adjustment and intelligence than girls in students of art faculty and self- concept in the students of science faculty and also mental health differs significantly while subject belonged to different gender and discipline of the study. Girls had greater security-insecurity feeling than boys in the students of arts faculty; greater emotional stability, adjustment and security-insecurity in the students of science faculty and emotional stability, autonomy and security-insecurity in the students of commerce faculty.

Garima Gupta and Sushil Kumar (2010) examined the relationship between mental health, emotional intelligence and self-efficacy among students. Results showed that emotional intelligence and self-efficacy are positively correlated with mental health. It also revealed that male students were better than female students in terms of mental health, emotional intelligence and self-efficacy which underline the importance of training in emotional intelligence, self efficacy and mental health for female college students.

Seyedeh Najmeh Noorbakhsh et al (2010) examined that Emotional intelligence and coping styles with stress The aim of this study was to examine the relationship between emotional intelligence and coping styles with stress in a sample of students. Four hundred and thirteen students (140 boys, 273 girls) were included in this study. All participants completed the Emotional Intelligence Scale (EIS) and the Tehran Coping Styles Scale (TCSS). The results revealed that EI was positively associated with problem-focused and positive emotional focused coping styles, and negatively associated with negative emotional focused coping style. EI is supposed to influence coping strategies through management and regulation of emotions, utilization and facilitation of emotions, and appraisal of emotions.

Jose Piqueras (2011) probed the relationship between emotional intelligence, the ability to cope with stressful events and sex differences were observed. Different studies show that high emotional intelligence levels are associated with coping strategies based on reflection and problem solving, while low levels are associated with coping strategies based on avoidance, rumination and superstition. Therefore, emotional intelligence plays an important role in the emotional self-control and the individual's adaptive capacity to cope with stressful situations. Different studies show that women pay more attention to emotions and are more empathetic, which is associated with a ruminate coping style focused on emotion, while men have higher levels of emotional self-regulation in stress situations.

Satdev Verma and Pushkrit Gupta (2011) studied emotional intelligence in relation to mental health and adjustment of secondary school students. The result of research revealed that correlation between emotional intelligence and mental health is significant and another correlation between emotional intelligence and adjustment also proved significant. The t-ratio regarding emotional intelligence between male and female is significant but after considering adjustment the result came to just opposite i.e., negative.

Brinda Sharma (2013) found that the relationship pattern and mental health in adolescents, results indicate that adolescents whose parents were viewed as accepting, especially the mother, had a better mental health status. Above average to average level of parental acceptance was found for adolescents belonging to high socio-economic status whereas average to below-average level of parental acceptance accounted for those belonging to low socio-economic status. Parental acceptance also differed significantly for boys and girls. High to above- average level of parental avoidance was seen among adolescents from high socio-economic background. Variance in paternal avoidance was indicated for boys and girls. The level of parental concentration was average for both groups. However, there is a difference in Mothers concentration towards boys and girls.

Mahmood Ahmad Khan and Nisar Ahmad Bhat (2013) studied to compare adolescent boys and girls on emotional intelligence. Adolescent boys are found to be more responsible, better able to make intelligent decisions using a healthy balance of emotions and reasons. Results revealed that the adolescent boys and girls differ significantly on composite score of their emotional intelligence

Rakesh Bharti (2013) investigated emotional intelligence as a source of personal power indispensable for success in today s world and managing stress. The present study aimed at exploring the relationship between emotional intelligence and achievement stress among the student-teachers. The investigator has taken emotional intelligence as a very important independent factor to see its effect on achievement stress of male and female student- teachers. The study was conducted on a sample of 600 student-teachers (Male=300 and Female=300) selected randomly form the 12 colleges of education, University of Jammu, Jammu. Collected data were analyzed using mean, S.D., ANOVA and Pearson s coefficient of correlation to test the hypotheses. Results of this study indicated significant differences between student-teachers possessing high and low emotional intelligence on achievement stress. Mean of high emotional intelligent student-teachers found significantly higher than low emotional intelligent student-teachers on achievement stress. A moderate positive and significant relationship exists between emotional intelligence and achievement stress of male and female student-teachers. Further it was also found that emotional intelligence and achievement stress are not mediated by gender.

Abdul Rahman Al Asmari (2014) investigated the effects of Emotional Intelligence on academic achievement of male and female English language undergraduates in Saudi Arabia. Various statistical processes were run to examine the relationship between Emotional Intelligence constructs, language competence, and academic achievement across genders. The responses were compared with their performance in English language tests. It was found that higher Emotional Intelligence levels of female undergraduates had positive impact on their performance in English language tests. Females also scored better in Emotional Intelligence constructs: intrapersonal, interpersonal, stress management and general good.

Ghosh (2015) explored gender differences in emotional intelligence among tribal and non-tribal adolescent school students of Tripura. Her study showed significant differences between tribal and non-tribal students on overall emotional intelligence. Further, she revealed gender differences in emotional intelligence among school students.

Bibi et al., (2016) proved a positive relationship between self-esteem and emotional intelligence among Pakistani university students. Using convenient sampling, the investigation was carried out on a sample size of 250 boys and girls of Islamabad universities. Results found that female students emerged as emotionally intelligent compared to their male counterparts.

Dharvinder Singh et al., (2016) studied emotional intelligence in relation to academic achievement of secondary school students. Emotional intelligence and academic achievement of 160 secondary school students (Male=80, Female=80) was examined. Emotional intelligence scale by Dhar, Hyde and Pethe (2002) was used to assess emotional intelligence and the marks scored by the students in the previous class were used to assess academic achievement. Demographic information was collected and Mean, SD, t-test and Pearson product moment correlation were calculated. No significant gender differences in emotional intelligence among students were found. Significant positive relationship was found between emotional intelligence and academic achievement among secondary school students.

Abiodun Musbau Lawal, Erhabor Sunday Idemudia & Tema Senyatsi (2018) investigated emotional intelligence (EI) influences on mental health indicators among students. Three hundred students (females = 50%; age range = 16 to 40 years, mean age = 20.10) participated in the study. The participants completed surveys on EI dimensions (well-being, self-control, emotionality, and sociability) and mental health indicators (somatic symptoms, anxiety, social dysfunction, and depression). Multivariate Analysis of Variance (MANOVA) revealed that students with high scores on well-being or emotionality EI dimensions tend to be higher in social functioning; while those with high scores in self-control or high in sociability EI dimensions tend to report fewer somatic and depressive symptoms, respectively. Post-hoc tests following MANOVA indicated that well-being and sociability EI dimensions interacted to reduce depressive symptoms, while well-being, emotionality, and sociability EI dimensions interacted to reduce both anxiety and depression. Well-being, self-control, emotionality, and sociability dimensions of EI appear significant for the mental health of students.

Asfandyar Fida et al., (2018) attempted to investigate emotional intelligence of students. Since there are differences in the findings of various studies in terms of gender; therefore, this study also considers exploring the discrepancy of the emotional cognizance of the male and female learners at university level. The outcomes of the investigation showed that female learners were ahead of male in emotional intelligence.

Ramana and Anitha Devi (2018) investigated the relationship between emotional intelligence and academic performance of Intermediate students. The sample of the study consisted of 300 second year Intermediate girl students of Krishna district, Andhra Pradesh.

The results indicated a positive correlation between emotional intelligence and academic achievement of students.

Jane Waithira Karimi, Jacinta Aswani Kwena & Alice Anika (2020) studied the relationship between emotional intelligence and academic achievement among students in Kilifi County. There was a strong positive relationship between emotional intelligence and academic achievement of the participants. Emotional intelligence domains were shown to relate significantly to academic achievement of the students.

Kumar (2020) conducted a study on the emotional intelligence of higher secondary school students. The result showed that emotional intelligence was independent of gender, subject, locality, type of family, father s occupation, and family income. The level of higher secondary school student s emotional intelligence was average in nature. The female students are better than the male students on their emotional intelligence.

Venkateswar Meher, Rajashree Baral and Sadhujan Bankira (2021) investigated the emotional intelligence scores of four-year integrated B.Ed. Trainees, to compare the emotional intelligence scores of four-year integrated B.Ed. Trainees, in terms of their sex, to compare the academic performance scores of students having high and low emotional intelligence scores and to investigate the relationship between the emotional intelligence scores and academic performance scores of students. The findings of the study revealed that about 6% of students had high emotional intelligence scores and 94% had above-average emotional intelligence scores. The study revealed no significant difference between the emotional intelligence scores of boys and girls. It was also found that the academic achievement scores of students having high emotional intelligence scores were more as compared to the students having low emotional intelligence scores. The study also reported a significant positive correlation between emotional intelligence and the academic performance of students.

Type of Management Vs Emotional Intelligence

Usha and Rekha (2009) conducted a study on emotional intelligence and mental health as predictors of academic achievement of students in Thrissur district of Kerala state. The sample consists of 530 in government and private college students. Emotional Intelligence Scale by Singh, Mental Health Status Scale by Gupta and Singh and Academic Achievement marks obtained by the previous academic year was taken into consideration. Findings suggested that male student teachers scores were higher on emotional intelligence, mental health and academic achievement than female student teachers; private college student teachers scored higher on emotional intelligence, mental health and academic achievement than government college student teachers and urban students scored higher on emotional intelligence, mental health and academic achievement than rural students.

Zeynep Kalyoncu et al., (2012) investigated emotional intelligence as one of the biggest factors that contribute to the success of individuals who assume various tasks and roles in modern life. It is also important in determining how individuals cope with the stress that can potentially limit their emotional relationships, decrease their efficiency, and reduce the pleasure of life. The main purposes of the present study were to consider the concepts of emotional intelligence and stress, and to conduct an applied study of the relationship between these two variables. The nurses who worked at some of the private and governmental hospitals in the province of Ankara were studied, and this present study identified a significant relationship between emotional intelligence and stress.

Atilgan Erözkan (2013) explored the relationship between perceived emotional intelligence and coping skills of undergraduate students. The present study was aimed at exploring the relationship between emotional intelligence and coping skills. The sample consisted of 691 (331 females; 360 males) undergraduate students who study different departments of the Faculties of Education and Technical Education, and department of physical education and sports teaching of School of Physical Education and Sports at Mugla Sitki Kocman University. Emotional intelligence levels and coping styles of undergraduate students were measured using the Bar-On Emotional Quotient Inventory (Bar-On, 1997) and the inventory of styles of coping with stress (Ozbay & Sahin, 1997). Pearson product-moment correlation analysis and structural equation modeling were employed to analyze data. Emotional intelligence was found to be significantly correlated with coping skills.

Viquar Unnisa (2020) assessed to find out the emotional intelligence among secondary school students. The emotional intelligence of students studying in schools of different managements i.e. Government schools with mean and standard deviation respectively were (81.55, 19.14), Private schools (93.9, 11.25), aided schools (85.2, 14.65), which is significant at (0.01). Furthermore, it was also revealed that all the groups in compare i.e. Government & private schools, Government & aided schools, and private & aided schools had shown significant differences among them. It is concluded that the selected schools, such as Government schools, private schools, and aided schools students had shown significant emotional intelligence differences among them.

Locality Vs Emotional Intelligence

Mahesh Bharvad (2015) aimed the emotional intelligence and adjustment among school students so investigator selected three groups one is type of faculty second is type of area and third is sex. Results indicated that there is significance difference between the urban and rural students for their emotional intelligence.

Mahmood Ahmad Khan and Mohammad Muzzafar Lone (2015) aimed to compare the emotional intelligence of rural and urban students of the age group of 20-25. The results revealed that there was no significant difference between the emotional intelligence (composite scores) of the rural and urban students but there is a significant difference between the two on factor-D (emotional stability) and factor-H (value orientation) of emotional intelligence.

Nature of Course Vs Emotional Intelligence

Fathima and Neelakandan (2011) tried to identify the human well being through Emotional Intelligence among the college going students. The sample consists of 100 college students from Arts and Science streams.

They were selected randomly. Emotional Intelligence Questionnaire as used to collect the data. t test proves that there is a significant difference between boys and girls in their emotional intelligence.

Makvana (2014) conducted as emotional intelligence in the variables associated as a Types of area's (rural and urban), types of a streams (Arts and Science), and types of sex as a male and female. The results revealed that rural student are more emotional intelligence than urban school students are. In addition, emotional intelligence has be found to the greater in student of science stream compare to arts student and female student's as compare to a student of arts stream and male student's respectively.

REVIEW OF RELATED STUDEIS ON ACADEMIC STRESS

Gender Vs Academic Stress

Yeh (1992) examined the Stress, coping, and psychological health of vocational high school nursing students associated with an academic examinations. An important issue for the nursing education system in Taiwan is to reinforce nursing education to enhance academic exams in nursing specialties. Consequently, to meet the prospective demands of technical manpower, not only do nursing students in college and vocational schools pursue further studies, using a descriptive cross-sectional design, the study examined the following among nursing students in vocational high schools, the subjects were 441 third-year nursing students of vocational high schools in northern Taiwan, recruited by convenience sampling. A significant interaction was observed between stress perceived and problem-focused coping used for psychological health at the lower and moderate stress levels (25 - 75%T) than that at the extreme stress level (> 75%). Conversely, emotion-focused coping had a negative main effect or impairing psychological health.

Distress, stress and coping in first-year student nurses. Levels of affective distress, sources of stress and coping strategies reported by first-year student nurses in Tayside, Scotland, were measured using the General Health Questionnaire (30-item version), the Beck and Srivastava Stress Inventory (BSSI) and a modified 'Ways of Coping Questionnaire'. Screening showed that around the time of an initial series of hospital placements, 50.5% of students in cohort 1 (n = 109, week 40) and 67.9% of students in cohort 2 (n = 111, week 24) suffered significant affective distress. This exceeds levels reported in published studies of degree nursing students, fourth-year medical students, and the general female population. Distressed students reported the same sources of stress as the non-distressed students, but suffered them more intensely. Many BSSI items were seen as common sources of stress; however, the frequency with which an item was reported to be stressful was not related to whether scores on that item predicted overall distress. In both cohorts, the use of direct coping was associated with lower levels of distress and with lower total stress scores on the BSSI. The use of fantasy and hostility was associated with high levels of distress and stress, in both groups. This screen of 220 first-year student nurses suggests that there is a problem with student distress around an initial series of general/surgical and psycho-social ward placements. The possible determinant of this distress and complex and it is unlikely that presenting information alone will be sufficient to reduce this distress (Jones and Johnston, 1997). Levels of academic related stress differed among male and female students with female students leaning towards high academic stress level than their male counterparts (Abouserie, 1994; Bang, 2009; Misra & Mckean, 2000).

Ranjitha and Michelle (2000) investigated the interrelationship among academic stress, anxiety, time management and leisure satisfaction among 249 college students by age and gender. Time management behaviors had a greater buffering effect on academic stress than leisure satisfaction activities. Significant gender differences existed among all the measures. Females had more effective time management behaviors than males, but also experienced higher academic stress and anxiety. Males benefited more than females from leisure activities. Freshmen and sophomore students had higher reactions to stress than juniors and seniors. Anxiety, time management and leisure satisfaction were all predictors of academic stress in the multivariate analysis. Anxiety reduction and time management in conjunction with leisure activities may be an effective strategy for reducing academic stress in college students.

Katyal, Sudha, Vasudeva and Pramila (2001) explore gender differences among adolescents in the areas of academic stress, parental attitude, parental aspirations, achievement motivation, intelligence, anxiety and attitude towards studies in a sample of 150 adolescents. Moderate to high academic stress was noted among all adolescents. Girls experienced significantly higher academic stress and anxiety than boys. Mothers were more authoritarian and less democratic towards girls than boys. Fathers had higher aspirations for boys than for girls.

Huan, Yeo, Ang, and Chong (2005) investigated the role of optimism together with gender, on students perception of academic stress. Four hundred and thirty secondary school students from Singapore participated in this study and data were collected using two self-report measures: the Life Orientation Test and the Academic Expectations Stress Inventory. Results revealed a significant negative relationship between optimism and academic stress in students. Gender was not a significant predictor of academic stress and no two-way interactions were found between optimism and gender of the participants.

Lauren A. Gentry et al., (2007) observed stress has been recognized as a public health problem. However, little research has been done on gender differences in sources of stress and coping strategies in Hawaii. A statewide cross-sectional telephone-survey of 1518 participants was conducted during the spring and summer of 2006. Women reported higher overall perceived stress levels, but there was no difference in the experienced social stressors and health stressors between genders. Men perceived more stress from personal factors. There were no gender differences in the perceived ability to cope with stress. However, women were more likely to use adaptive coping strategies, whereas men were more likely to use maladaptive and avoidance coping strategies. There were no significant gender differences in stages of change for stress management. Based on this study, interventions can be developed to help people better cope with stress. Interventions for women may focus on increasing the use of adaptive strategies such as praying and talking to friends and family, while interventions for men may introduce the use of adaptive coping strategies such as exercise and actively fighting causes of stress. This study shows that gender differences in stress levels and coping in Hawaii are similar to previous studies conducted on the mainland. More research into specific stressors and coping strategies may help tailor interventions that are more effective and comprehensive.

Pau et al. (2007) concluded that the higher levels of academic stress among female students can be attributed to negative appraisals and focus on the emotional challenges in the wake of the stressful event. Conversely male students are trained to display strength and machismo in the face of challenges right from their young age. This implies that male and female students might be experiencing academic stress but they differ in their way of expression.

Singh and Upadhyay (2008) investigated academic stress in the context of age and sex differences among college students. The sample of the study was first year and third year male and female students (N= 400). Findings revealed that first year students experienced higher degree of academic stress in comparison of third year students. At the same time female students perceived more academic stress in comparison of their male counterpart.

Studies related to gender, type of management and locality with regard to level of academic stress. Levels of academic related stress differed among male and female students with female students leaning towards high academic stress level than their male counterparts (Abouserie, 1994; Misra & Mckean, 2000, Bang, 2009).

Bhupinder Pal Singh (2011) investigated the interrelationship among academic stress, anxiety, time management, and leisure satisfaction among 249 university undergraduates by age 120 and gender. Time management behaviors had a greater buffering effect on academic stress than leisure satisfaction activities. Significant gender differences existed among all the measures. Females had more effective time management behaviors than males, but also experienced higher academic stress and anxiety. Males benefited more than females from leisure activities. Freshmen and sophomore students had higher reactions to stress than juniors and seniors. Anxiety, time management, and leisure satisfaction were all predictors of academic stress in the multivariate analysis. Anxiety reduction and time management in conjunction with leisure activities may be an effective strategy for reducing academic stress in college students.

Boludola Owolabi (2013) examined students experienced academic stress resulting from test-taking, studying for examinations, grade competition, completion of assignment, and workload among others. Inability to manage stress effectively results in prevalence of failure, poor performance, truancy, drop-outs, lack of motivation, feeling of inadequacy, frustration and dejection among students. In view of this, emotional intelligence training was considered for managing academic stress under this study. This study is, thus, aimed at investigating the impact of emotional intelligence training on academic stress and self- efficacy among senior secondary school students. The study adopted pre-test, post-test, control group quasi experimental study with 2 × 2 factorial matrix comprising experimental and the control group by the row and gender vary at two levels-male and female in the column. The treatment package was scheduled for eight weeks based on the model of emotional intelligence developed by Bar-on (2002). Stratified random sample was used to select 140 participants into the experimental and control groups.

Ramesh Singh Bartwal and Anoj Raj (2013) investigated the most successful people do have an incisive mind, backed by high quality training as well as a host of good ideas. But if all this is coupled with Emotional Intelligence, the chances of their unmatched performance are very high. The present study was aimed at examining the relationship between academic stress and emotional intelligence of school going adolescents. The sample consisted of 200 students (100 urban and 100 rural area), further subdivided into 50 male and 50 female students in these areas. The data were collected from different senior secondary schools of District Bathinda (Punjab). The investigation revealed that the academic stress experienced by both male and female adolescents is similar, high score on Emotional Intelligence can deal in a better way with the academic stress.

Alireza Momeni, Behnam Makvandi and Zahra Bonabi Mobaraki (2014) investigated the present research is aimed to investigate the relationship between emotional intelligence, social support, coping strategies and stress of students of Ramhormoz City. The statistical population included all the students of Ramhormoz City, out of which a sample of 356 individuals

(182 male students and 174 female students) was selected through random stratified sampling. The data gathering tools included emotional intelligence, coping strategies and social support questionnaires. The research employed a correlation method. Multivariate regression and Pearson correlation coefficients were used to analyze the data. The results indicated that there exists significant difference between emotional intelligence, social support and coping strategies. Moreover, results of regression analysis indicated that the variable of emotional intelligence is the best predictor of the criterion variable of stress and coping strategies.

Anbumalar et al., (2017) examined that the study is gender difference in the perceived level of stress and coping strategies among college students. It establishes the context and the significance of the research being conducted by summarizing current understanding and background information about the topic, stating the purpose of the work in the form of research problem supported by hypothesis or a set of questions, briefly explaining the methodological approach used to examine the research problem highlighting the potential outcomes the study can reveal. Stress is a natural physiological mechanism that protects humans from danger. When stress occurs, the human body prepares for quick action by releasing hormones that increase alertness and focus. However, if the source of stress does not disappear, stress hormones can persist in the body. Continual exposure to stress hormones has been linked to a wide range of physical and psychological illnesses, such as obesity, gastrointestinal disorders, cardiovascular disorders, skin disorders, anxiety attacks, and depression. Results found that females showed higher rates on perceived stress level than males among college students.

Jayasankara Reddy, Karishmarajanmenon and Anjanathattil (2018) employed a quantitative research design where participants were screened using Academic Stress for streams namely, commerce, management, humanities, and basic sciences. The five dimensions of sources such as personal inadequacy, fear of failure, interpersonal difficulties with teachers, teacher pupil relationship and inadequate study facilities were further analysed and gender differences were also obtained.

Mishra and Manju (2018) found the level of academic stress among male and female students doing B.Ed. A Total of 50 students between 22-35 years of age range of B.Ed., section participated in the study. Among them 30 were male students and 20 were female students. Academic stress scale was used to measure the stress level of students. Result revealed that B.Ed., Students experience higher level of academic stress. Gender difference was also found to be significant as female students experienced lesser academic stress than male students.

Ravi (2018) found that boys have experienced more stress than girls. Students studying urban colleges have experienced more Stress than rural.

Students with good study habits have experienced more stress than poor study habits. Students with low intelligence have experienced more stress than high intelligence.

Saleh Alsulami et al., (2018) aimed to measure the level of academic stress and to determine its risk factors in students enrolled in HSPP-adapted local universities in Saudi Arabia. This study has found mean SAAS score for two local universities with competition-based versus non-competition-based HSPP learning models. Academic stress correlation with age, gender and universities was discussed.

Laigong Beatrice Chemutai and Shikuku M. Mulambula (2020) determined the influence of gender, type of university, year of study and age on the level of stress among university students in Kenya. The findings revealed a significant dissimilarity in the level of academic stress between male and female students. Female students were found to have higher stress level than the male students. The levels of stress also differed on the basis of the year of study with student in year three having higher levels of academic stress than those in the other years of study. Age and the type of university did not evident any significant influence on academic stress level. The study concluded that gender and the year of study significantly determined the level of academic stress among university students in Kenya. This study recommended that female students require more academic mentorship and be equipped with more stress coping mechanisms.

Type of Management Vs Academic Stress

Rao (2007) investigated on Stress and Coping Strategies among Adolescent Students, reported that gender has significant impact on academic stress of the adolescent students. Type of college also has significant impact on their academic stress.

Husain, Kumar and Husain (2008) explored the level of academic stress and overall adjustment among Public and Government high school students and also to see relationship between the two variables academic stress and adjustment). Results indicated that magnitude of academic stress was significantly higher among the Public school students where as Government school students were significantly better in terms of their levels of adjustment. However, inverse but significant relationships between academic stress and adjustment were found for both the group of students and for each type of school.

Vishnu Vardhana Rao and Laxmanaiah (2011) stated that Students of both Government and Private Schools were found to have a similar stress perception. The students of Government- run schools exhibited more of avoidance coping strategies and therefore suitable for a systematic study on chronic stress for early intervention.

Subramani and Kadhiravan (2017) revealed the link between academic stress and mental health among students. Significant difference in mental health of students from private and government schools was found. He asserted that students from private schools have a different nurturing and vast exposure as compared to government school students who belong to poor socio economic background and lack of exposure.

Chandan and Shivappa (2020) made an attempt to review the existing literature on academic stress experienced by the higher secondary school students and tried to find the causes and stressors of academic stress as well as the coping strategies for academic stress. The author concludes that the support system and conducive environment is much required for the students to advance in their academic life and for reaching greater heights and goals.

Aswartha Reddy & Lalitha (2021) focused on academic stress among adolescent students in Government and Corporate Colleges. Gender wise results showed that male subjects are higher Stress compare to female subjects. The type of college indicated that the mean for the government colleges have experience low stress than corporate college. Also type of college wise results showed that corporate colleges are high stress compare to Government colleges.

Kiran Pal Singh Chawla and Archana Agrawal (2021) found that the higher secondary students are having moderate level of academic stress and irrespective of sub samples of the higher secondary students are having moderate level of academic stress. Male and female students do not differ significantly in their academic stress scores. Rural and urban area students do not differ significantly in their academic stress scores. Government and private school students do not differ significantly in their academic stress scores.

Locality Vs Academic Stress

Dewan (2003) studied on a sample of 769 students found that students with average academic stress were more emotionally stable as compared to the students having high academic stress. Further found that family stress of students belonging to both urban and rural areas affect their academic achievement.

Kavitha (2011) studied the academic, psychological and general stress and adjustment among rural and urban college students. A quasi experimental between group design and purposive sampling was used for the study. The sample included both male and female students, belonging to rural and urban background. It was hypothesized that there will be a correlation between stress and adjustment in students; there will be a significant difference in stress and adjustment among rural and urban students. The students were screened on General Health Questionnaire

(Goldberg & Hillier, 1972) and were administered Stress Response Checklist (Verma, 1997) and Adjustment Inventory for College Students (Sinha & Singh, 1995). The assessment tools were scored and results obtained. Analysis of results were done by using correlation for the scores on stress and adjustment, t was computed for the scores on stress and adjustment of rural and urban students. Results indicated a significant level of stress both psychological and academic, among the rural based students than their counterparts in the urban areas.

Zeynep Kalyoncu et al., (2012) probed the relationship between emotional Intelligence and stress caused by the Organization: a study of nurses. Emotional intelligence is one of the biggest factors that contribute to the success of individuals who assume various tasks and roles in modern life. It is also important in determining how individuals cope with the stress that can potentially limit their emotional relationships, decrease their efficiency, and reduce the pleasure of life. The main purposes of this study were to consider the concepts of emotional intelligence and stress, and to conduct an applied study of the relationship between these two variables. The nurses who worked at some of the private and governmental hospitals in the province of Ankara were studied, and this present study identified a significant relationship between emotional intelligence and stress.

Sahana Madhyastha, Latha and Asha Kamath (2014) investigated medical school is challenging as medical students have to confront varied stressors such as academic pressures, work over load, and issues pertaining to professional competence. Stress can be more during the final year of study as students have to deal with pressure of graduating and making career decisions. Efficient coping protects students against stress. Gender differences may exist in stress and coping. The present study aimed to examine stress, coping and gender differences in final year medical students. Prediction of stress by coping was also examined. This cross-sectional study consisted of 117 final year medical students from a medical college in coastal Karnataka. Professional Student Stress Survey to measure stress and Carver s Brief COPE to measure coping were administered. An almost similar amount of mild and moderate degree of stress was experienced by majority of the sample. Academic performance and professional identity issues caused greater stress. Among the major coping approaches, problem coping was used more by the group. The coping sub types frequently used were planning, active coping, acceptance, and self-distraction. There were no gender differences in stress. With regard to coping, females used more emotional coping strategies, specifically, self-blame and seeking emotional support. Venting, an emotional coping strategy repeatedly emerged as a positive predictor of overall stress and various stress domains. Positive re-framing negatively predicted stress and religion positively predicted stress in two stress domains respectively. The findings point towards the crucial need for stress management programs in medical school. Though students used problem coping frequently, the evident role of maladaptive coping in increasing stress warrants the need for coping skills training. Research on effectiveness of such programs in India needs to be improved.

Razia (2016) observed that adolescents of private schools have more academic stress than their counterparts in government schools.

Shycil Mathew (2017) showed that, most of the urban subjects (83.3%) had severe academic stress and 16.7% of them had very severe academic stress, whereas in the rural area all the subjects had moderate academic stress. Most of the urban subjects (98.3%) coping was moderate and 1.7% subjects had good coping. There was no significant association of academic stress scores and coping strategies scores of urban and rural adolescents and selected demographic variables.

Snehlata Ghatol (2017) made the academic stress among the secondary school students and presents the causes and symptoms of stress as well as coping mechanism for stress. The review of literature indicate that the reasons for stress during adolescence are because of disturbed family dynamics, peer pressure, inability to cope with studies, drug abuse, lack of competence. The involvement of adolescents in getting instant gratification of needs has led to lot of stress in them and in their relationships with family and peers. The students coming from joint families have slightly higher mean of academic anxiety score than their counterparts coming from nuclear families but this difference is not significant statistically. Proper care should to be taken in helping to take the right decisions which may affect their future. Anxiety reduction and time management in conjunction with leisure activities may be an effective strategy for reducing academic stress in college students. Students should have the aspiration/expectation about their study, not beyond their capacities and abilities, Students need also proper counselling while selecting their courses at intermediate level. The family environment should be congenial and the learning process should be made pleasurable and parents should avoid making it as a stressful event for adolescents.

Shycil Mathew (2017) showed that, most of the urban subjects (83.3%) had severe academic stress and 16.7% of them had very severe academic stress, whereas in the rural area all the subjects had moderate academic stress. Most of the urban subjects (98.3%) coping was moderate and 1.7% subjects had good coping. There was no significant association of academic stress scores and coping strategies scores of urban and rural adolescents and selected demographic variables.

Ravi (2018) found that Boys have experienced more stress than girls. Students studying urban colleges have experienced more Stress than rural.

Students with good study habits have experienced more stress than poor study habits. Students with low intelligence have experienced more stress than high intelligence.

Umar, Usman Sani (2019) revealed that significant difference between academic stress of male and female students and no significant difference in academic stress of rural and urban location school students.

Chandan and Shivappa (2020) made an attempt to review the existing literature on academic stress experienced by the higher secondary school students and tried to find the causes and stressors of academic stress as well as the coping strategies for academic stress. The author concludes that the support system and conducive environment is much required for the students to advance in their academic life and for reaching greater heights and goals.

Kiran Pal Singh Chawla and Archana Agrawal (2021) found that the higher secondary students are having moderate level of academic stress and irrespective of sub samples of the higher secondary students are having moderate level of academic stress. Male and female students do not differ significantly in their academic stress scores. Rural and urban area students do not differ significantly in their academic stress scores. Government and private school students do not differ significantly in their academic stress scores.

Nature of Course Vs Academic Stress

Ruth Lo (2002) investigated the perception and sources of stress, coping mechanisms used, and self-esteem in nursing students during 3 years of their undergraduate nursing programme. The sample consisted of a cohort of nursing students going through 3 years of a nursing programme. The method was a descriptive correlation design. Results indicated that students in year 1 experienced significantly less transient stress as compared with year 2; students in year 3 had more positive self-esteem than year 2 students. There were no significant differences with regard to chronic stress, avoidance and proactive coping, and negative self-esteem. The four main stressors in the last three years for this cohort of students, in descending order are nursing studies, finance, family and health. They coped by using both problem-focused and emotion-focused coping skills. There is a need to review the nursing curriculum and evaluate what impacts on students' stress levels, and also introduce strategies to reduce the stress levels of nursing students.

Akgun and Ciarrochi (2003) hypothesized that highly resourceful students would be more effective than others at protecting themselves from the adverse effects of academic stress, and not allowing that stress to impact their grades. A sample of 141 first-year undergraduate students completed measures of academic stress and learned resourcefulness. Their first-year GPAs were obtained from university records. Analysis revealed that academic stress was negatively associated with academic performance. High academic stress adversely impacted the grades of low resourceful students but had no effect on high resourceful students.

Singh and Singh (2008) conducted a study on Stress and adjustment among professional and non-professional students. Stress in modern life leads to several poor emotional adjustment among the professional students. The present study was carried out to compare the stress and emotional adjustment of students of professional courses. They were administered on ESQ by Kapoor Bhargav India adaptation and Bell Adjustment Inventory Indian adaptation by S. Hussain to assess for stress and adjustment. The main findings were professional students have more stress. The result also indicated that professional students were poorly emotionally adjusted in comparison to non-professional group. Professional students have more stress as compared to non-professional students. Psychological intervention inform of therapy will help these students to help well.

Robert et al., (2009) investigated involving a group of 290 medical and dental students to directly compare perceived stress levels encountered during their education. The purpose of the investigation was to determine if the sources of stress reported by medical and dental students, both male and female, were dueto common factors. A multivariate statistical analysis was also conducted to measure stress differences by year in school. Through factor analysis, the survey question responses were grouped into five causal categories: academic performance, faculty relations, patient and clinic responsibilities, personal life issues, and professional identity. The overall findings show that dental students had greater levels of stress than medical students in three of the five categories. The only category in which medical students demonstrated greater stress levels than dental students was in professional identity. Measures of comparative levels of stress between male and female students for either profession did not demonstrate any significant differences. Stress levels related to clinical work varied significantly between the type of professional student and his or her year in school.

Sukhpal Kaur et al., (2009) examined that Stress and coping in the nursing students. The purpose of the present study was to identify the stressors and coping strategies of baccalaureate nursing students at one of the premier institutes of the country. A total of 205 nursing students undergoing graduation were taken up for the study. The research instrument used was a self-administered questionnaire to identify the various causes of stress and the coping strategies they were using to overcome these stresses. Major stressors identified were academic in nature followed by social, personal, financial and family causes. Coping strategies used were hobbies and leisure time activities, self-care, seeking social support and maladaptive ones such as (crying, isolating self, and avoiding recalling stressful events). It is inferred from the present study that by understanding the various stressors amongst the nursing students and by exploring how they cope with their difficulties will provide the building block for further interventions designed to minimize the stress amongst them.

Elzubeir, Elzubeir and Magzoub (2010) carried a study to provide a systematic review of studies reporting on stress, anxiety and coping among Arab medical students and to identify implications for future research. Search strategy used combinations of the terms: Arab medical student, stress, PBL, psychological distress, depression, anxiety and coping strategies. Within the limited range of Arab medical students studied, suggests that these students have a high prevalence of perceived stress, depression and anxiety, with levels of perceived psychological stress as high as those reported in the international literature for medical students of other regions of the world. Limited data were available regarding coping strategies, the impact of stress on academic performance and attrition among Arab students. No data were available regarding the impact of problem-based learning on stress and coping. It was concluded that stress, depression and anxiety are common among Arab medical students, as for students elsewhere. Little is known about the contribution of different curricula approaches to perceived stress and what coping strategies institutions and students apply to help alleviate stress.

Mannapur et al., (2010) observed that the students with psychological stress were found to be involved in habits like tobacco chewing and smoking, as well as alcohol intake. Average stress of the professional group is significantly higher than non-professional group of students.

Supe (2010) investigated in a study determined incidence of stress and factors controlling stress in medical students at various stages of MBBS course at Seth G S Medical College. 238 students (First year 98, Second 76, Third 64) were asked to complete a questionnaire on personal data (gender, stay at hostel, mode of travel, time spent in travel every day, medium of study in school, place of school education.), Stress inducing factors, Zung's depression scale, ways of coping, stress relievers, perceived social support and personality type. Statistical tests used were ANOVA, critical ratio and Student s t test. Results revealed that majority of medical students (175/ 238-73%) perceived stress. Stress was found to be significantly more in Second and Third MBBS students rather than First MBBS levels ($p<0.05$). Stress was not found to differ significantly on the basis of sex, stay at hostel, model of travel, time spent in travel every day, medium of study in school, place of school education. Stress was found to be significantly more in students having more than 95% of marks at 12th Standard as compared to others. Academic factors were greater perceived cause of stress in medical students. There was no significant difference in the students at different levels of MBBS regarding academic factors and social factors as a stress inducing factors. Emotional factors were found to be significantly more in First MBBS students as compared to Second and Third MBBS students. Stress in medical students is common and is process oriented. Academic factors are greater perceived cause of stress in medical students at Seth G S medical college. Emotional factors are found to be significantly more in First MBBS. It is dependent on person's ways of coping and social support.

Balkishan Sharma et al., (2011) conducted a study on academic stress and its effect on vital parameters in final year medical students at SAIMS Medical College, Indore, Madhya Pradesh. Stress can reduce the efficiency of healthy individuals and it has been shown in most of the physiological studies. The present study was carried out to assess stress and its effect on vital parameters during academic examination in final year medical students. The study was carried out at Sri Aurobindo Institute of Medical Sciences, Indore. The final MBBS students of academic year 2010-11 were selected for study. The height, weight, pulse rate and blood pressure were taken before and during examination. Zung s scale was used for assessment of Stress. Out of 71 students 68 participated in the study. There was highly significant difference in vital parameters [Pulse rate ($t=8.89$, $P<0.001$), Systolic Blood Pressure ($t=3.89$, $P<0.001$) and Diastolic Blood Pressure ($t=2.86$, $P<0.006$)] during examination. It was also observed that the stress level was high. SDS Index of stress was more in girls as compared to boys. No significant change was observed in weight. It was observed that academic examinations for medical students are stressful and produce changes in vital parameters which may affect their academic performance. Girls had more stress as compared to boys. Academics and examinations are the most powerful stressors in medical students.

Bishakha Majumdar (2011) studied the nature of the academic stress among university students and the relation between academic stress and several demographic, academic and socio-cultural factors. Data was collected from 350 students studying at the postgraduate level in the University of Calcutta – from both science and humanities stream. Data was collected using a specially designed General Information Schedule, Stress Inventory for Students in Higher Education, Rosenberg Self Esteem Scale and the Warwick Edinburgh Mental Well Being Scale. The findings indicated a negative relation between academic stress and mental health; with high self-esteem being predictive of positive mental health and adaptive coping strategies. Institutional variables such as teaching style, equipments and facilities and opportunities for career development were found to be related to academic stress. Since interventions mostly focus on psychological guidance and counselling, the acceptability of psychological interventions among students were investigated - revealing only a limited acceptability among students for mental health services.

Charanjeev Singh, Sunita Sharma and Ravinder Kumar Sharma (2011) investigated the level of stress and coping strategies used by nursing interns. The effects of stress on nursing students have been well documented. High perceived stress levels and lack of effective coping skills could be a barrier to achieve the challenges of profession. Keeping this in mind, a study was conducted to find out the level of stress and coping strategies used by nursing interns of National Institute of Nursing Education, PGIMER, Chandigarh. A self- administered Stress scale, Perceived stress scale, Scale of Physic psycho social response to stress and scale to assess the coping strategies were developed and validated with the help of experts in the field of nursing, psychology, Public Administration and Psychiatry. Data was collected by administering all the scales to nursing interns after taking informed written consent from them. Results showed that two third of interns had moderate to severe stress, especially during their clinical practice. Students were found to cope up stress by using various coping strategies like avoidance, transference, problem solving and optimism. It is recommended that to have stress reduction among students, nurse educators should find out the most stressful areas and give a serious thought to encourage the use of healthy coping strategies to improve the productivity of students in nursing.

Bhavin et al., (2012) studied the components of academic stress among the Masters of Business Administration students of GTU affiliated colleges. Many researchers have identified the components of academic stress and different stressors which impact the students. This study further tries to enlighten each component of academic stress such as curriculum and instruction, team work related issues, assessment, and placement, impact on performance and outcomes of Academic stress. Three major stressors have been identified which affect the performance and three major outcomes of stress. Around twelve micro issues have been identified under the curriculum and instruction component while three stressors were prioritized related to team work; seven sub issues regarding assessment and three micro issues under placement components of academic stress. The sample comprises of 118 Masters of Business Administration students of GTU affiliated colleges from all the five zones of Gujarat.

Sanjeev Kumar and Bhukar (2013) investigated the stress levels and coping strategies of professional students belonging to Physical Education and Engineering professions. A sample of 60 subjects was randomly selected from the Physical Education and Engineering Institute, India. Each profession group had 30 subjects (15 boys and 15 girls) with age range of

21±3 years. Stress scores due to: 1) frustration and inhibition, 2) overload and 3) compulsive, time-urgent and aggressive behavior were measured for the selected subjects using the questionnaire developed by Daniel et al. (1979). The second questionnaire developed by George and Everly and used by Heyward (1991) was also administered to the students to measure their coping strategy. Two way analysis of variance (ANOVA) showed that stress due to all the stimuli was significantly higher among girls in comparison to boys of their profession. Coping strategy was higher in boys than girls of their respective profession, but Physical Education girls had higher coping strategy than boys and girls of Engineering. Therefore, it can be concluded that Physical Education students had better coping strategy than engineering students.

Prabu (2015) researched on the higher secondary students and implied that male students are more stressed than the female students. Urban students academic stress is greater than the rural students. Government school student s stress is low than the private school student s stress. Students from Science stream are more stressed than the students from Arts.

Ramaprabou, Dash and Sasi Kanta (2018) conducted to find out the effect of academic stress on achievement motivation of college students. 50 college students of various professional, arts, and science colleges functioning in and around Puducherry were approached at random to collect data using purposive sampling method. Academic stress scale developed and standardized by Rajendran and Kaliappan (1990) and Achievement Motivation Scale by Pratibha Deo and Asha Mohan (1985) were used for data collection. The collected data were statistically analysed using „t test and one way ANOVA. The findings revealed that moderate stress leads to high achievement motivation.

Ali Khanehkeshi and Basavarajappa (2012) suggested that the study has investigated the relationship of academic stress, depression and self-efficacy with academic performance among high school boy students. Using a random stratified sampling technique, 120 students from three academic grades including 1st grade, 2nd grade, and 3rd grade, were selected. The findings of the study was the relationship among academic stress, depression and self-efficacy have a simple and multiple significant correlations to academic performance. There is a significant difference between academic grades in terms of academic stress, depression and academic performance.

The present study conducted by Suvarna (2014) concerned with the stress management and Emotional intelligence of 378 students studying B.Ed., in Mandya district. A two points scale to asses Stress management and five points scale to asses Emotional intelligence was used. The results revealed that 8.20% of B.Ed students showed high level of stress management. And 25.66% of B Ed students showed high level of emotional intelligence. There is negligible negative correlation between Stress management and Emotional intelligence of B.Ed. students.

NEP-2020:

The NEP 2020 paves for numerous significant changes in the Indian education system. The changes and objectives of NEP 2020 are as follows:

1. School Education

- The current **'10+2'** structure covering ages 6-18 to be replaced by a new Pedagogical and Curricular Structure of **'5+3+3+4'** corresponding to ages 3-18.
- Instead of annual examinations every year, students will now only attend exams in Class 3, 5 and 8.
- Class 10 and 12 Board Exams will be conducted as usual, but the exams will be made easier by allowing students to **take exams twice** a year. The exam will have two parts, Objective and Descriptive.
- Universal standards of learning and regulations in public and private schools.
- Vocational Education and coding will be introduced from Class 6.
- Mother tongue or regional language to be the medium of instruction at least up to Class 5 and preferably till Class 8.
- Report cards will be a **360-degree Holistic Progress Card** that will give a comprehensive report on skills and capabilities instead of just marks and grades
- Focus on the curriculum to core concepts.
- **Universalization** of education from Early Childhood Care Education (ECCE) to Secondary Level.
- Achieving **100% Gross Enrolment Ratio** (GER) in school education by 2030.
- New National Curriculum Framework for Early Childhood Educator (ECE), schools, teachers and adult students.
- **Open Schooling System** to bring two crore 'Out Of School Children' back into the mainstream.
- Deployment of counselors and social workers to improve student's mental health.

CONCLUSION

The related study on Emotional Intelligence and Academic stress are reviewed and categorized as Gender versus emotional intelligence, Type of management versus Emotional Intelligence, Locality vs Emotional

Intelligence, Nature of school vs emotional intelligence, Gender vs Academic stress, type of management vs Academic stress, Locality vs Academic stress, Nature of course vs academic stress. In view of findings of the studies the researcher made an attempt to select certain important variables, i.e sociological variables and psychological variables that are supported by many other studies. Review of literature reveals that an extensive study of the influence of emotional intelligence and academic stress are very rare. It is an attempt to see the relationship between academic stress and emotional intelligence. The area under investigation is novel and unexplored one with respect to population of Intermediate students. The need for research on such study is warranting.

CHAPTER 3

Methodology

INTRODUCTION

The present section of methodology illustrates research approach and design considered of current study. It has been noted as a endeavor towards the process of elucidating as well as justifying apt more of research design in terms of apprehending a problem of research. It is the source to employ the collection of data as well as techniques to attain analysis of data. Methodology is subject to connection between research problem and the procedure by which this problem can be analyzed. This section has been categorized under to distinctive parts. These are implication of types of data, the method of research and the in-depth analysis of collected data.

This chapter on methodology offers an overview about the research design, types of data collected, sampling design and relevant interpretation towards the conduct of research, statistical tools selected for proposed hypothesis of the research. Methodology adopted for the study is described under the following headings.

- Method of study
- Variables of the study
- Tools used for data collection
- Sample of the study
- Procedure of data collection
- Statistics used for data analysis

METHOD OF STUDY

Remmer has observed - "Since no two research under takings are exactly alike it is impossible to set forth any rigid formulation of methods of procedure. There is a wild variation in the conditions and circumstances which determine the objective nature of research problems in different fields. The purpose of the study may vary from researcher to researcher in terms of where it is to be conducted and applications that are to be made of it. In addition, great difference in the capacities and characteristics among the individuals who do research work are a proved fact". Agarwal (1975)

There are three basic categories in the educational research methods. They are:

1. Historical method
2. Experimental method
3. Survey method.

Historical method

It describes what was the process involved in investigating, recording, analyzing, and interpreting the events of the past. This is usually accomplished by an interpretation of the events and of their relevance to present circumstances and what might happen in future.

The main purpose of historical research therefore, is to arrive at an acute account of the past so as to gain a clear perceptive of the present. The knowledge enables us to predict and control our future existence.

Experimental method

This method is oriented towards the discovery of basic relationships among phenomena as a means of predicting and eventually controlling their occurrence. According to John W. Best, experimental research is the description and analysis of what will be, or what will occur, under carefully controlled situation (Best, 1963). Experiment has proved to be an essential and powerful tool leading man towards progress.

Survey method

Best (1982) rightly said, "The survey is an importance type of research. It must not be confused with the mere clerical defined routine of gathering and tabulating figures. It involves clearly defined problems and definite objectives. It requires expert and imaginative planning, careful analysis and interpretation of the data gathered and logical and skillful reporting of the findings". It describes and interprets what adjusts at present. Best has preferred to use the term "Descriptive research". The main purpose of this research is to study, describe and explain present phenomena, their status and their trends, to form the basis for planning and formulation of policies, to form the basis of fundamental research.

The "Survey method" of descriptive research was followed by the researcher in the present study. The investigator felt that this method was appropriate for the present investigation.

DESIGN OF THE STUDY

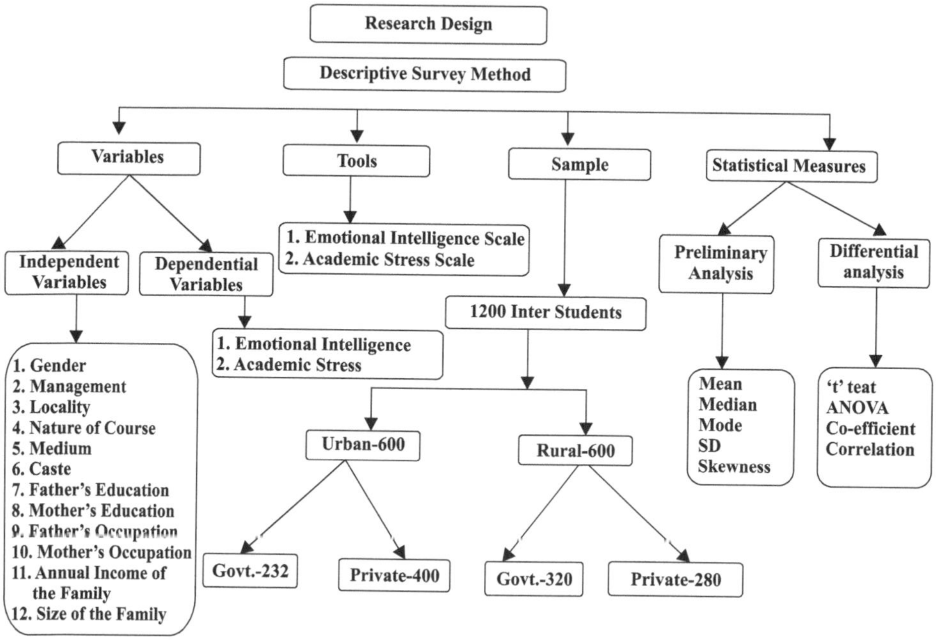

VARIABLES OF THE STUDY

In this study the following variables were taken in to consideration.

A. Dependent variables:

1. Emotional Intelligence
2. Academic Stress

B. Independent variables

I. Socio-Demographic variables.

1. Gender
2. Management
3. Locality
4. Nature of Course
5. Medium
6. Caste
7. Mother s Education
8. Father s Education
9. Mother s Occupation
10. Father s Occupation
11. Annual Income of the Family

12. Size of the Family
13. Type of the Family

TOOLS USED FOR THE STUDY

In the present investigation the researcher selected the following tools for the purpose of data collection.

1. Emotional Intelligence scale developed and standardized by Nutankumar Thingujam, and Usha Ram (1999).
2. Academic Stress scale developed and standardized by Kumar reddy B.S (1999).

Description of the Tools

Emotional Intelligence Scale: The Emotional Intelligence of the Subjects was assessed by using Emotional Intelligence Scale developed by Nutankumar Thingujam, and Usha Ram (1999). It consists of 33 items. Each question has 5-Options. The Items are scored with the help of Scoring key. The reliability of the instrument 0.90 was established by test-retest method and the validity is 0.78.

The Emotional intelligence scale was scored by giving weightages to the responses 5, 4, 3, 2 and 1. The maximum score 165 and minimum score 33 obtained by adding the weightages on all these items. Appropriate coding is given to the response given to personal variables.

Academic Stress Scale

Students Academic Stress Scale was developed and standardized by Kumar Reddy B.S (1999). It consisted of 40 items and sub divided into five components having eight items in each category. 1. Personal inadequacy (F1), 2. Fear of failure (F2), Interpersonal difficulties with teachers (F3), 4.Teacher/pupil relationship/teaching methods (F4) and 5. Inadequate study facilities (F5).

Students Academic Stress scale was score by giving weightages to the responses 0-1-2-3 and 4. The Maximum score 160 and Minimum score 40 obtained by adding the weightages on all these items.

This scale was adopted and revised by the researcher and used in this investigation.

Preparation of academic Stress scale

(*i*) Exactly 75 statements were first prepared in Telugu, the regional language of the subject on whom it had to be used and got translated in to English by respective language experts. This was done to facilitate students to give the correct response. Care has been taken to frame the items in simple and unambiguous language.

(*ii*) The clarity and consistency in ideas were scrutinized by the subject experts and the expression and style was checked by language specialists.

(*iii*) Preliminary form of questionnaire was again checked by the express for suitability, vocabulary used grammatical errors. Clarity in meaning, size of the letters used in the items, time factor needed. Spelling mistakes if any.

(*iv*) On the suggestions of the subject experts language specialists and students some of the items were modified and rephrased. After editing the items carefully 10 items were deleted on the advice of the experts and 65 items are retained which were suitable to measure the students academic stress scale of intermediate students.

(*v*) Each item of the inventory was arranged on a 5 point scale with responses: No Stress, Slight Stress, Moderate Stress, High Stress and Extreme stress.

Pilot study: The Telugu version was administered to a small group of intermediate 2nd year students. A separate answer sheet is used. The student is asked to write any one of the appropriate letters namely A, B, C, D and E in the bracket given against the respective level of stress statement number. They were also asked to answer the items and identify the language difficulties. The words marked by them which could not understand were modified or substituted with simple words. Thus the constructed students academic stress scale was used to measure the academic stress of intermediate students.

Item analysis: The Telugu version of the students academic stress scale was administered on a representative sample of 200 students studying intermediate 2nd Year, selected at random from 4 colleges representing in Prakasam district and also considering the gender. The inventory was administered in small groups. Sufficient time was given to the students in order to respond properly.

The item analysis is an important statistical procedure. The investigator differentiates good items from the poor ones. Every item of a test should contribute something towards the measurement of the attribute on hand. Otherwise, it does not serve any purpose except lengthening the test. Hence the suitability of the items has to be thoroughly checked while preparing the test.

(a) All the 200 scripts were arranged in the descending order of the level of stress scores obtained by the students on students academic stress scale.

(b) The top 27% (50) scores of scripts and bottom 27% (50) scores of scripts were separated and grouped in to five categories according to the responses strongly agree and so on, against the first statement.

(c) Scale value and frequencies of each of the response say No Stress, Slight Stress, Moderate Stress, High Stress and Extreme stress etc., were noted.

(d) The mean (M) and standard deviations (SD) for the top 50 scripts were computed.

(e) Similarly, the mean (M) and standard deviations (SD2) for the bottom 50 scripts were also computed.

(f) The same procedure was adopted in the case of other statements of students academic stress scale.

Out of 40 items in the final study, there are 6 negative items. The items 4, 9, 16, 26, 29 and 34 are negative. The remaining items (34) are positive. The r values for all the items of the pilot study of students academic stress scale are presented in Table 3.1.

Table 3.1: The Pearson s correlation coefficient values for all the items of the pilot study of Students Academic Stress Scale

Item No.	r values	Remarks
1.	0.425	Retained
2.	0.286	Retained
3.	0.062	Retained
4.	0.093	Retained
5.	0.104	Retained
6.	0.149	Retained
7.	0.379	Retained
8.	0.235	Retained
9.	0.021	Retained
10.	0.006	Retained
11.	0.108	Retained
12.	0.461	Retained
13.	0.591	Retained
14.	0.113	Retained
15.	0.091	Retained
16.	0.278	Retained
17.	0.274	Retained
18.	0.441	Retained
19.	0.341	Retained
20.	0.419	Retained

21.	0.450	Retained
22.	0.044	Retained
23.	0.328	Retained
24.	0.529	Retained
25.	0.223	Retained
26.	0.376	Retained
27.	0.335	Retained
28.	0.486	Retained
29.	0.479	Retained
30.	0.467	Retained
31.	0.262	Retained
32.	0.375	Retained
33.	0.517	Retained
34.	0.365	Retained
35.	0.426	Retained
36.	0.590	Retained
37.	0.108	Retained
38.	0.601	Retained
39.	0.273	Retained
40.	0.608	Retained

Standardization of Academic Stress Scale

The scores obtained for students academic stress scale was tabulated and r is computed for the differences of mean scores. The value of r is found to be 0.551 which is highly significant. Hence, the tool is considered as valid.

The final students academic stress scale is prepared after deleting the invalid items (5) in the preliminary inventory. The final version of the students academic stress scale has consisted of 40 items.

For the final study out of 40 items, there are 6 negative items. The items 4, 9, 16, 26, 29 and 34 are negative. The remaining items (34) are positive.

Scoring Procedure

In the case of the students academic stress scale Likert s scoring technique was adopted. For each attitude statement, a scale value was assigned as shown in the below Table 3.2.

Table 3.2: Numerical values for different alternatives of the positive and negative items

Alternatives	Scale Value	
	Positive items	Negative items
No Stress	0	4
Slight Stress	1	3
Moderate Stress	2	2
High Stress	3	1
Extreme stress	4	0

The total score of each on students academic stress scale was indicated on the top of the answer sheet.

Reliability

Reliability is the most indispensable characteristic of any measuring instrument. It refers to the consistency of scores obtained by the same individuals at different occasions or with different sets of equivalent items.

Traditionally, the text books have told us that there are three fundamental types of approach to the estimation of reliability. All of these were designed to answer the question, what is the self-correction of this test. There have been three standard procedures known as the split-half, alternative forms and test-retest methods (Guilford, 1954).

A tool is said to be reliable if it reveals similar results in various situations. The test-retest and parallel form methods of estimating reliability may be common and legitimate for both power and speed tests. In the power test, each student has enough time to respond to correct answer. Speed test usually yields spuriously high reliability co-efficient when split-half and internal consistency methods rut employed (Stanley et al., 1978).

Split-Half Reliability

By means of this technique, which is used to find internal consistency the items in a whole test were divided into two halves which should he equivalent or very nearly so. Thus, the two scores, one for each half, one obtained for each individual by administering the test only once and each score is treated as though it is represented a separate form" (Freeman, 1965).

It is sometimes called co-efficient of equivalence. The test is split into two equivalent halves usually by pooling the odd numbered items for one half, whereas the even numbered items for the second half of the test. This usually makes the two scores obtained from a single test reasonable equivalent. By applying the Pearson correlation co-efficient for the half test is 0.551. It shows that the reliability of the instrument is very high.

Test- Retest Reliability

The reliability of the students academic stress scale is also computed using Test-Retest Method on a sample of 200 with a gap of 20 days for retest. The Test-Retest Reliability of the students academic stress scale is 0.551.

Validity

"A term which indicates a validity referring not to what a test actually measure but to what it appears, on the basis of a subjective evaluation, to measure of all the concepts of validity, the least justifiable, valuable in the original writing of test items" (Good, 1973).

Face Validity

It is a "measure of the degree to which a test appears to be valid, while this is the most superficial kind of validity, it may contribute significantly to the legitimacy of the test in the eyes-of the candidates" (Madhu Raj, 1996).

If a common thread of achievement runs through all the items of the test. The resultant test has "face validity". All the items in the students academic stress scale have a common thread of measuring students academic stress. So, there is face validity in students academic stress scale.

Construct Validity

Construct Validity of test measures particular characteristics of an individual. If a test can indicate the individual's actual achievement of instructional objectives, it is valid from the construct point of view.

Construct validity is "Validity evaluated by investigating what qualities a test measures, that is by determining the degree to which certain explanatory concepts or constructs account for performance on a test" (Good, 1973).

Hence, there is construct validity for student s academic stress scale.

Concurrent Validity

In a situation of some observable criterion, the scale's validity can be investigated by seeing how good an indicator it is. This approach leads to two categories of validity, i.e., 'predictive validity' and 'concurrent validity'.

Concurrent validity is a 'validity based upon correlation with a criterion variable, that is, by determining the degree to which certain explaining concepts or constructs account for performance on the test" (Good, 1973).

Predictive Validity

Predictive validity is concerned with how the scale forecast a future criterion and concurrent validity with how well it can describe a present one. Good defined it as validity based upon correlation with a criterion variable that is not available until sometime after testing (as, for example, school grades). Predictive validity can be 'obtained by giving a test to a group of subjects and then comparing the test results with the job performance of those tested.

Predictive validity is one type of validity most strongly advocated by the EEOC. Because, predictive valid tests are excellent indicators of future performance (Madhu Raj, 1996).

The results in the succeeding chapter show that students academic stress scale has both concurrent validity and predictive validity.

POPLATION AND SAMPLE OF THE STUDY

Intermediate students studying in Guntur, Prakasam and Nellore districts of Andhra Pradesh state constituted the population of the study. There are 1900 girls students and 1200 boys students. So, the total population of 3100 Intermediate students constituted the study.

Among 3100 Intermediate students 1200 students are selected randomly as sample of the study. Four government and private colleges located in urban and rural areas of the each of the above districts were selected randomly. After selection of the colleges, 2nd year intermediate students from Arts and Science groups of these colleges are selected randomly.

The stratified random sampling was applied in three stages, in the first stage; gender (Boys: 572 Girls: 628), management of the college (Government: 632 & Private: 568) in second stage and third nature of course (Arts Group 580 & Science Group: 620) intermediate students are included in this study. The total sample of the study is 1200.

Sample Design

Nature of Course	Gender				Total
	Boys		*Girls*		
	Management		Management		
	Government	*Private*	*Government*	*Private*	
Arts	130	160	140	150	**580**
Science	160	140	150	170	**620**
Total	**290**	**300**	**290**	**320**	**1200**

Sample Characteristics based on Gender

Gender influences the emotional intelligence of students. Both male and female were considered for the study to examine whether there is any significant different between the two sexes in their emotional intelligence and academic stress.

Sample Characteristics Based On Management

Private and government college students differ in so many respects. Under the present study management is taken as one of the variable to see if there is any difference between the two management students in Emotional Intelligence and academic stress.

Sample Characteristics based on Locality

Urban and rural college students are differing in so many respects like behaviour, attitude, personality, interest. From this point of view the variable locality was included in this investigation.

Sample Characteristics based on Nature of Course

Arts and Science group students are differing in so many respects like attitude and their interest. From this point of view the variable Nature of Course was included in this investigation.

Sample Characteristics based on Medium of Instruction

English and Telugu medium student differ in so many respects like reading, writing, speaking, using the language etc. Both English and Telugu medium students were considered for the study to examine whether there is any significant difference between the two group of students on emotional Intelligence and academic stress.

Sample Characteristics based on Caste

OC, BC, and SC/ST Students are taken for determining influence of caste on emotional intelligence ability and academic stress of Intermediate students.

Sample Characteristics based on Mother's Education

Student's fathers having different educational qualifications are taken for determining influence of father's education on emotional intelligence and academic stress.

Sample Characteristics based on Father's Education

Student's mothers having different educational qualifications are taken for determining influence of father's education on emotional intelligence and academic stress.

Sample Characteristics based on Mother's Occupation

Mothers with different occupations are taken for determining influence of mother's occupation on emotional intelligence and academic stress of students.

Sample Characteristics based on Father's Occupation

Fathers having different occupations are taken for determining influence of father's occupation on emotional intelligence and academic stress of students.

Sample Characteristics based on Annual Income of the Family

On the basis of the information obtained from the subjects through a personal data sheet, the sample is divided into two groups on the father's income and mother's income and the family income to study whether there exists any significant difference between the two groups of children in their emotional intelligence and academic stress.

Sample Characteristics based on Type of the Family

Students which heiring up to 3, 4-6 and above 6 family members are taken for determining emotional intelligence and Academic stress of students.

Sample Characteristics based on Birth Order

Different birth order students have been taken for determining influence of Birth order on emotional intelligence and Academic stress of students.

Sample Characteristics Based on Size of the Family

Students which haring Below 5, 5 to 10, above 10 family members are taken for determining influence on emotional intelligence.

PROCEDURE OF DATA COLLECTION

The investigator conducted the tests in two sessions. At first the researcher approached the college management/principals with a written request to collect data from the students. Then the investigator personally contacted the intermediate college students as per the schedule given by the college management. After establishing rapport with the students, two questionnaires namely emotional intelligence scale and students academic stress scale were administered with necessary instructions. In the first session, the investigator distributed the emotional intelligence scale to group of 20 students and they were explained the instructions in greater detail and their responses were obtained in a separate answer sheet. In the second session the investigator distributed the students academic stress scale to the same subjects and obtained their responses in separate answer sheets.

STATISTICS USED FOR DATA ANALYSIS

On the basis of the objectives of the investigation, statistical is carried out by employing appropriate statistical techniques. Frequency distribution tables prepared for attitude towards moral values for all the groups. Mean, Median. Mode, Range, Quartile Deviation, Standard Deviation, Skewness, Kurtosis, Coefficient of Variation and Standard Error of Mean were calculated wherever necessary. The significance tests like t test, F test and correlation were employed. Multiple R was calculated by carrying out step-wise regression analysis to predict the emotional intelligence and academic stress among intermediate students. For dividing the groups, quartile values and Sten values were used whichever is necessary. All the above calculations were done by using the SPSS software.

The obtained numerical results were adumbrated by graphical representations. The significant levels employed with respective symbols are given below.

The testing of formulated hypotheses of present study has been taken up in the following chapter.

CHAPTER 4

Analysis and Interpretation of Data

INTRODUCTION

This chapter deals with analysis and interpretation of data. The data resulting from any study or visually a collection of observations or measurements. Simple direct inspection of data cannot ascertain valued conclusions about the study. Statistical analysis provides valued inferences about the data and helps the investigator to make accurate conclusions about the study. In the present study the relevant data collected work the Emotional Intelligence and Academic Stress test scores of Intermediate students studying in various management colleges of Andhra Pradesh state. The analysis of data is presented as follows:

- Preliminary Analysis
- Differential Analysis

PRELIMINARY ANALYSIS

The frequency distribution tables of intermediate students for their Emotional Intelligence and Academic Stress scores are presented in the following pages.

Frequency distribution of emotional intelligence scores for the whole group

The investigator measured emotional intelligence scores of intermediate students using Emotional Intelligence (EI) scale developed and standardized by Nuthan Kumr Thingujam & Usharam.

It is a five point scale, five alternatives i.e. Strongly Agree, Agree, Doubtful, Disagree and Strongly Disagree. The minimum and maximum score of Emotional intelligence scale are 33 and 165 respectively. Frequency distribution of emotional intelligence among students for the whole group is presented in the Table 4.1.

The Distribution characteristics namely Mean, (M). Median (Mdn), Mode (Mo), Range ®, Standard Deviation (SD), Skewness (Sk), Kurtosis (Ku) and Standard Error of Mean (SEM) are also presented in Table 4.1.

Table 4.1: Frequency distribution table for Emotional Intelligence scores of Intermediate students

S. No.	Class Interval	Limits	Mid Point	F	CF	CPF
1.	81-90	81.5-90.5	86	22	22	1.83
2.	91-100	91.5-100-5	96	45	67	5.58
3.	101-110	101.5-110.5	106	203	270	22.5
4.	111-120	111.5-120.5	116	295	565	47.08
5.	121-230	121.5-130.5	126	315	880	73.33
6.	131-140	131.5-140.5	136	254	1134	94.5
7.	141-150	141.5-150.5	146	42	1176	98
8.	151-160	151.5-160.5	156	24	1200	100

N=1200

Mean (M) = 125.52 Standard Deviation (SD) = 14.42
Median (Md) = 126.00 Skewness (Sk) = 0.231
Mode (Mo) = 125.50 Kurtosis (Ku) = 0.135
Range (R) = 93.00 Standard Error of mean (SEM) = 0.41

It is observed from table 4.1 that the mean of emotional intelligence score is 125.52. There are 33 items in the emotional intelligence scale. The neutral value of the scale is 99 (33 × 3 =99). The Mean of emotional intelligence score is far greater than the neutral value. Hence, it is concluded that intermediate students have positive emotional intelligence.

The values of Skewness (Sk) and Kurtosis (Ku) are 0.231 and 0.135 respectively. For the normal distribution the values of Skewness (Sk) and Kurotosis (Ku) are 0.00 and 3.00 respectively. Hence, the frequency distribution is positively skewed and platy kurtic.

The Bar diagram for the distribution of emotional intelligence scores for the whole group is given in Figure 4.1.

The frequency Polygon for the distribution of emotional intelligence scores for the whole group is given in Figure 4.2.

The Ogive curve for the distribution of emotional intelligence scores for the whole group is given in Figure 4.3.

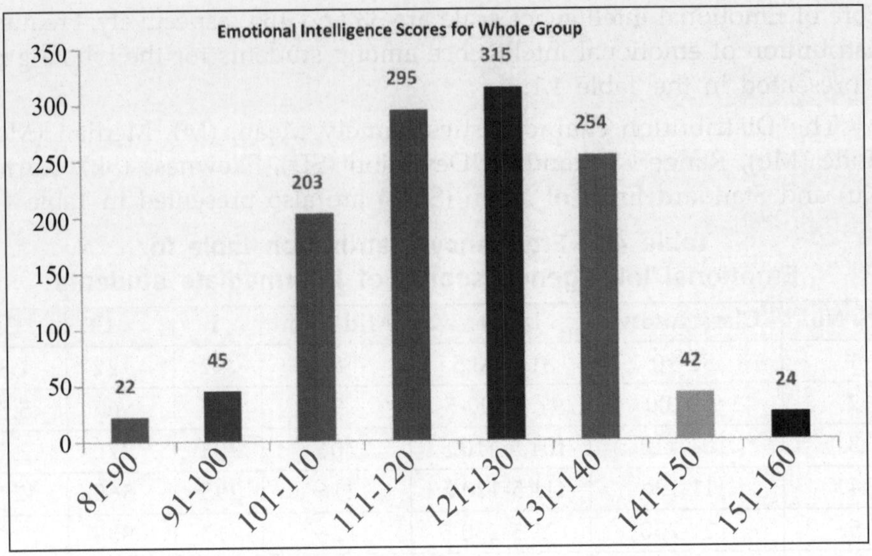

Fig. 4.1: Bar Diagram for the distribution of emotional intelligence scores of whole group.

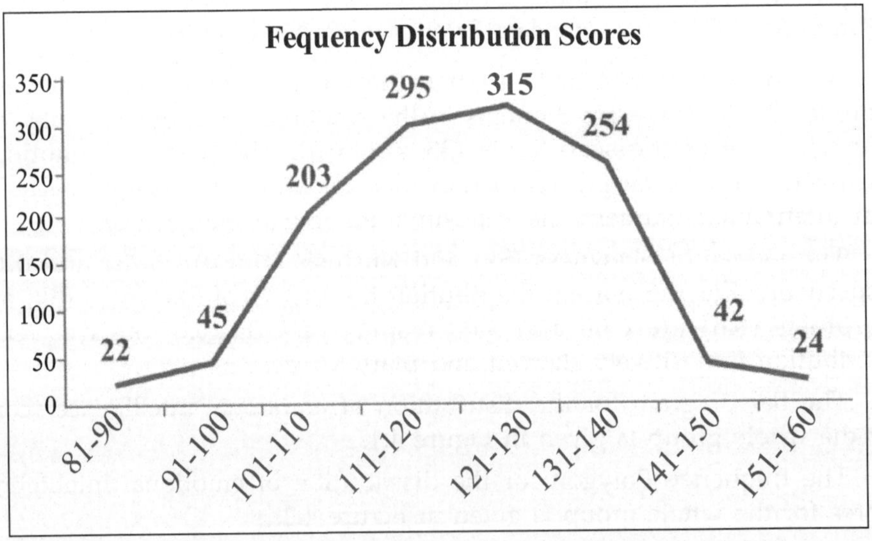

Fig. 4.2: The frequency polygon for the distribution of emotional intelligence scores of whole group.

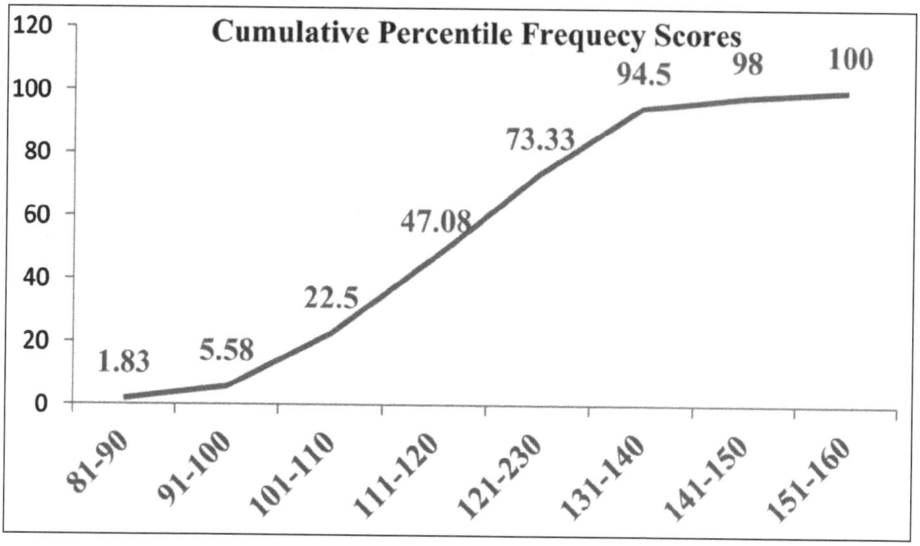

Fig. 4.3: The Ogive curve for the Frequency distribution of emotional intelligence of whole group.

Frequency distribution of academic stress scores for the whole group

The investigator measured Academic Stress score of the intermediate students by using Academic Stress (SASS) Scale developed and standardized by Kumar Reddy and Srinivas (1999).

The Academic Stress score is the total score on all the items (40 items) of the scale. It is a five point scales with five alternative responses, No Stress-0, Slight Stress-1, Moderate Stress-2, High Stress-3 and Extreme Stress-4. The minimum and maximum scores on Academic Stress scale are 40 and 160 respectively.

The Distribution characteristics namely Mean, (M). Median (Mdn), Mode (Mo), Range ®, Standard Deviation (SD), Skewness (Sk), Kurtosis (Ku) and Standard Error of Mean (SEM) are presented.

Frequency distribution of Academic Stress among students for the whole group is presented in the Table 4.2.

It is observed from Table 4.2 that the mean Academic Stress is 122.27. There are 40 items in the Students Academic Stress Scale. The neutral value of Academic Stress scale is 120 (40 × 3 =120). The Mean Academic Stress score is far greater than the neutral value. Hence, it is concluded that the intermediate students have positive academic stress.

Table 4.2: Frequency distribution table for Academic Stress scores of the whole group

S. No.	Class Interval	Limits	Mid Point	F	CF	CPF
1.	76-85	75.5-85.5	80.5	39	39	3.25
2.	86-95	85.5-95.5	90.5	47	86	7.16
3.	96-105	95.5-105.5	100.5	108	194	16.17
4.	106-115	105.5-115.5	110.5	280	474	39.5
5.	116-125	115.5-125.5	120.5	295	769	64.08
6.	126-135	125.5-135.5	130.5	276	1045	87.08
7.	136-145	135.5-145.5	140.5	113	1158	96.5
8.	146-155	145.5-155.5	150.5	42	1200	100

N=1200

Mean (M) = 122.27	Standard Deviation (SD) =16.18
Median (Md) = 122.00	Skewness (Sk) = -0.261
Mode (Mo) = 111.00	Kurtosis (Ku) = -0.131
Range (R) = 88	Standard Error of mean (SEM) = 0.46

The values of Skewness (Sk) and Kurtosis (Ku) are -0.261 and -0.131 respectively. For the normal distribution the values of Skewness (Sk) and Kurtosis (Ku) are 0.00 and 3.00 respectively. Hence, the frequency distribution is negatively skewed and platy kurtic

Bar diagram for the distribution of Academic Stress scores of the whole group is given in Figure 4.4.

The frequency Polygon for the distribution of Academic Stress scores of the whole group is given in Figure 4.5.

The Ogive curve for the distribution of Academic Stress scores of the whole group is given in Figure 4.6.

DIFFERENTIAL ANALYSIS

Provides inferences involving determination of statistical significance of difference between groups with reference to selected variables. The influence of the variables gender, management, locality and their interaction effects on emotional intelligence and academic stress of intermediate students is studied with the help of factorial design. The three way ANOVA is used to determine if there is an interaction effect between three independent variables on a continuous dependent variables.

In the present study the influence of gender, management and locality on emotional intelligence and academic stress is investigated by employing 2 × 2 × 2 factorial design.

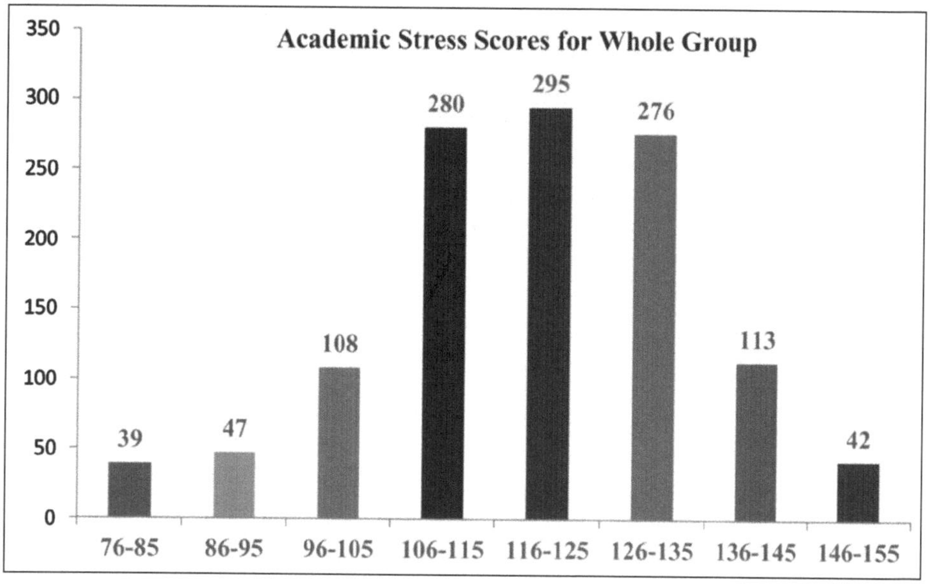

Fig. 4.4: Bar Diagram for the distribution of Academic Stress scores of the whole group

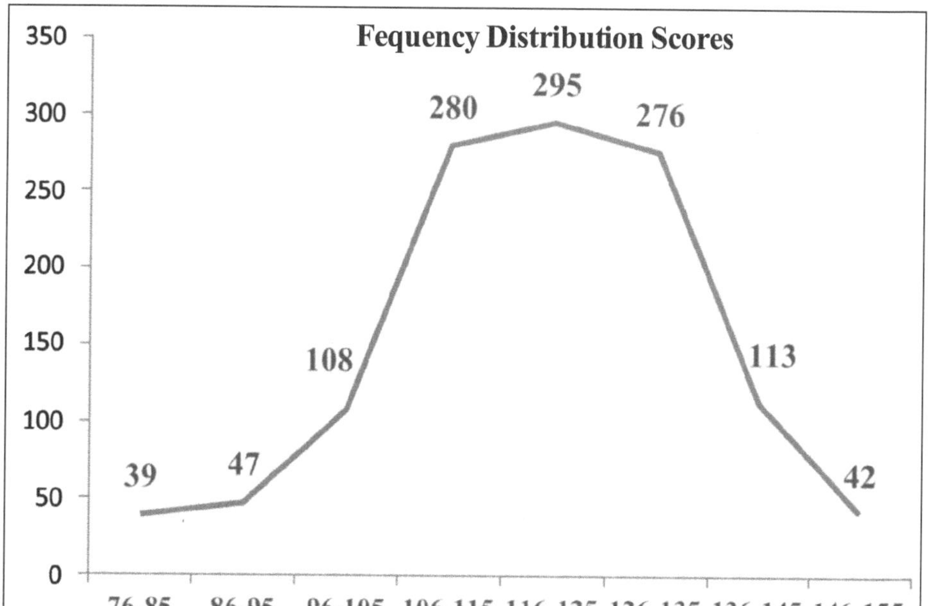

Fig. 4.5: The frequency polygon for the distribution of Academic Stress scores for the whole group

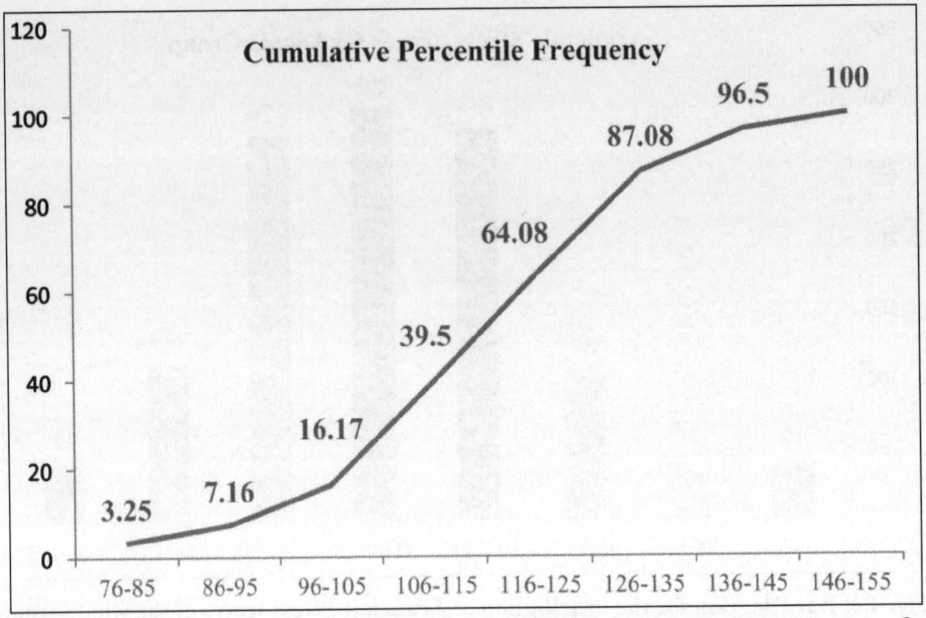

Fig. 4.6: The Ogive curve for the Frequency distribution of Academic Stress scores for the whole group

HYPOTHESIS-1

There would be no significant influence of the main effects of gender, management and locality on emotional intelligence and academic stress of intermediate students.

HYPOTHESIS-2

There would be no significant impact of interaction effect of gender, management and locality on emotional intelligence and academic stress of intermediate students.

To test the above hypotheses, Analysis of Variance (ANOVA) technique is employed using 2 × 2 × 2 factorial design and the results are presented in Table 4.3.

It is evident from Table 4.3(b) that the main effect gender has significant influence at 0.01 level on emotional intelligence among intermediate students. The calculated F value for the variable gender (12.95) is greater than the table value 6.64 for 1 and 1192 df. Hence, Hypothesis-2 is rejected and concluded that gender has significant influence on emotional intelligence of intermediate students.

Table 4.3(a): Mean and SD for emotional intelligence scores under 2 × 2 × 2 (gender, management and locality)

Locality		Gender			
		Boys		*Girls*	
		Management		Management	
		Government	*Private*	*Government*	*Private*
Rural	Mean	**118.45**	123.73	126.49	130.84
	SD	13.85	14.38	13.83	13.73
Urban	Mean	123.46	127.09	130.96	**132.04**
	SD	13.79	13.23	13.21	13.69

Table-4.3(b): Results of Analysis of Variance (ANOVA) for emotional intelligence scores under the 2 × 2 × 2 (gender, management and locality) Factorial Design

Factor-A: Gender (2 levels)
Factor-B: Management (2 levels)
Factor-C: Locality (2 levels)

Source of Variance	Sum of Squares	df	Mean	F-Values	Level of Significance
Gender (A)	2438.101	1	2438.101	12.95	**
Management (B)	1294.668	1	1294.668	6.89	**
Locality (C)	1220.541	1	1220.541	6.84	**
A × B	375.201	1	375.201	7.30	**
A × C	950.688	1	950.688	5.05	*
B × C	1842.641	1	1842.641	9.78	**
A × B × C	1396.401	1	1396.401	7.42	**
Within	224462.620	1192	188.308	–	–
Total	249711.859	1199	–	–	–

**- Significant at 0.01 level
*- Significant at 0.05 level

The results of present study corroborate with the earlier findings of Petrides and Adrian Fumham (2000), Ciarrochi, Chan, and Bajgar (2001), Saroj (2003), Rabindra Kumar (2005), Patil and Kumar (2006) and Bindu & Immanuel (2006) which reported that gender has significantly influenced the emotional intelligence of students.

The computed F value for the main effect namely management is 6.89, it is greater than the table value of F (6.64) for 1 and 1192 df at 0.01 level of significance. Therefore, Hypothesis-2 is rejected for the main effect of management. Hence, it is concluded that management has significant influence on emotional intelligence among intermediate students.

The computed value F for the main effect namely locality is 6.84, it is greater than the table value of F (6.64) for 1 and 1192 df at 0.01 level of significance. Therefore, Hypothesis-1 is not accepted for the main effect of locality. Hence, it is concluded that locality has significant influence on emotional intelligence of intermediate students.

The computed value of F for the two factor interaction effect namely gender Vs management on emotional intelligence among intermediate students is 7.30. It is greater than table value of (6.64) for 1 and 1192 df at 0.01 level of significance. Therefore, Hypothesis-2 is not accepted. Hence, it is concluded that there is significant interaction effect of gender Vs management on emotional intelligence among intermediate students.

The computed value of F for the two factor interaction effect namely gender Vs locality on emotional intelligence of intermediate students is 5.05. It is greater than table value (3.84) for 1 and 1192 df at 0.05 level of significance. Therefore, Hypothesis-2 is not accepted and it is concluded that there is significant interaction effect of gender Vs locality on emotional intelligence of intermediate students.

The computed value of F for the two factor interaction effect namely management Vs locality on emotional intelligence among intermediate students is 9.78. It is greater than table value of (6.64) for 1 and 1192 df at 0.01 level of significance. Therefore, Hypothesis-2 is not accepted. Hence, it is concluded that there is significant interaction effect of management Vs locality on emotional intelligence among intermediate students.

The computed value of F for the three factor interaction effect namely gender Vs management Vs locality on emotional intelligence among intermediate students is 7.42. It is less than table value of (6.64) for 1 and 1192 df at 0.01 level of significance. Therefore, Hypothesis-2 is not accepted. Hence, it is concluded that there is significant interaction effect of gender (vs) management (vs) locality on emotional intelligence of intermediate students.

It is evident from Table 4.4(b) that the main effect of gender has significant influence at 0.01 level on the Academic Stress among intermediate students. The calculated F value for the variable gender (17.00) is far greater than the table value 3.84 for 1 and 1192 df at 0.01 level of significance. Hence, Hypothesis-1 is rejected and concluded that gender has significant influence on the Academic Stress among intermediate students.

Table 4.4(a): Mean and SD for Academic Stress scores under the 2 × 2 × 2 (gender, management and locality)

Locality		Gender			
		Boys		*Girls*	
		Management		**Management**	
		Government	*Private*	*Government*	*Private*
Rural	**Mean**	**132.13**	118.70	130.86	127.91
	SD	15.01	15.10	16.96	18.59
Urban	**Mean**	117.83	116.85	127.39	115.96
	SD	14.84	15.33	18.14	21.19

Table 4.4(b): Results of Analysis of Variance (ANOVA) for Academic Stress scores under the 2 × 2 × 2 (gender, management and locality) Factorial Design

Factor-A: Gender (2 levels)
Factor-B: Management (2 levels)
Factor-C: Locality (2 levels)

Source of Variance	Sum of Squares	df	Mean Square	F-Values	Level of Significance
Gender (A)	4933.041	1	4933.041	17.00	**
Management (B)	1336.741	1	1336.741	4.60	*
Locality (C)	589.901	1	589.901	2.03	@
A × B	1660.081	1	1660.081	5.72	*
A × C	493.021	1	493.021	1.70	@
B × C	445.308	1	445.308	3.11	@
A × B × C	595.021	1	595.021	2.50	@
Error	345884.793	1192	290.172	–	–
Total	355937.907	1199	–	–	–

**- Significant at 0.01 level
*- Significant at 0.05 level
@-Not significant at 0.05 level

The computed value F for the main effect namely management is 4.60, it is greater than the table value of F (3.84) for 1 and 1192 df at 0.05 level of significance. Therefore, Hypothesis-1 is not accepted for the main effect of management. Hence, it is concluded that management has significant influence on Academic Stress among intermediate students.

The computed value F for the main effect namely locality is 2.03, it is less than the table value of F (3.84) for 1 and 1192 df at 0.05 level of not significance. Therefore, Hypothesis-2 is accepted for the main effect of locality. Hence, it is concluded that locality has no significant influence on Academic Stress among intermediate students.

The computed value of F for the two factor interaction effect namely gender Vs management on the Academic Stress among intermediate students is 5.72. It is greater than table value of (3.84) for 1 and 1192 df at 0.05 level of significance. Therefore, Hypothesis-2 is not accepted. Hence, it is concluded that there is significant interaction effect of gender Vs management on Academic Stress among intermediate students.

The computed value of F for the two factor interaction effect namely gender Vs locality on the Academic Stress among intermediate students is 1.70. It is less than table value of (3.84) for 1 and 1192 df at 0.05 level of not significance. Therefore, Hypothesis-2 is accepted. Hence, it is concluded that there is no significant interaction effect of gender Vs locality on Academic Stress among intermediate students.

The computed value of F for the two factor interaction effect namely management Vs locality on the Academic Stress among intermediate students is 3.11. It is less than table value of (3.84) for 1 and 1192 df at 0.05 level of not significance. Therefore, Hypothesis-2 is accepted. Hence, it is concluded that there is no significant interaction effect of management Vs locality on Academic Stress among intermediate students.

The computed value of F for the three factor interaction effect namely gender Vs management Vs locality on the Academic Stress among intermediate students is 2.50. It is less than table value of (3.84) for 1 and 1192 df at 0.05 level of not significance. Therefore, Hypothesis-2 is accepted. Hence, it is concluded that there is no significant interaction effect of gender Vs management Vs locality on Academic Stress of intermediate students.

The Influence of Socio-demographic and Psychological Variables

The influence of socio-demographic variables, Gender, Management, Locality, Nature of Course, Medium of Study, Caste, Father s Education, Mother s Education, Fathers Occupation, Mothers Occupation, Annual Income of the Family, Size of the Family and Type of the Family on Emotional Intelligence and Academic Stress of intermediate students is investigated and considered for analysis.

HYPOTHESIS-3

There would be no significant influence of gender on Emotional intelligence and academic stress of intermediate students.

In the present investigation, the influence of gender on emotional intelligence and academic stress of intermediate students is investigated. The corresponding emotional intelligence and academic stress scores of boys and girls are analyzed accordingly. The influence of gender on the emotional intelligence and academic stress is investigated through t-technique.

The above hypothesis is tested by employing t-technique. The results are presented in Tables 4.5 and Table 4.6 respectively.

Table 4.5: Mean, SD. and t values for Emotional intelligence of Intermediate Boys and Girls.

S.No.	Gender	N	Mean	SD	't' Value	df	Level of Significance
1.	Boys	572	121.18	13.91	10.87	1198	**
2.	Girls	628	129.83	13.63			

** - Significant at 0.01 level

It is evident from the above table that the computed value of t (10.87) is greater than the table/critical value of (1.96) at 0.01 level of significance. Hence, Hypothesis-3 is accepted for the variable gender it is concluded that gender has significant influence on the emotional intelligence of intermediate students.

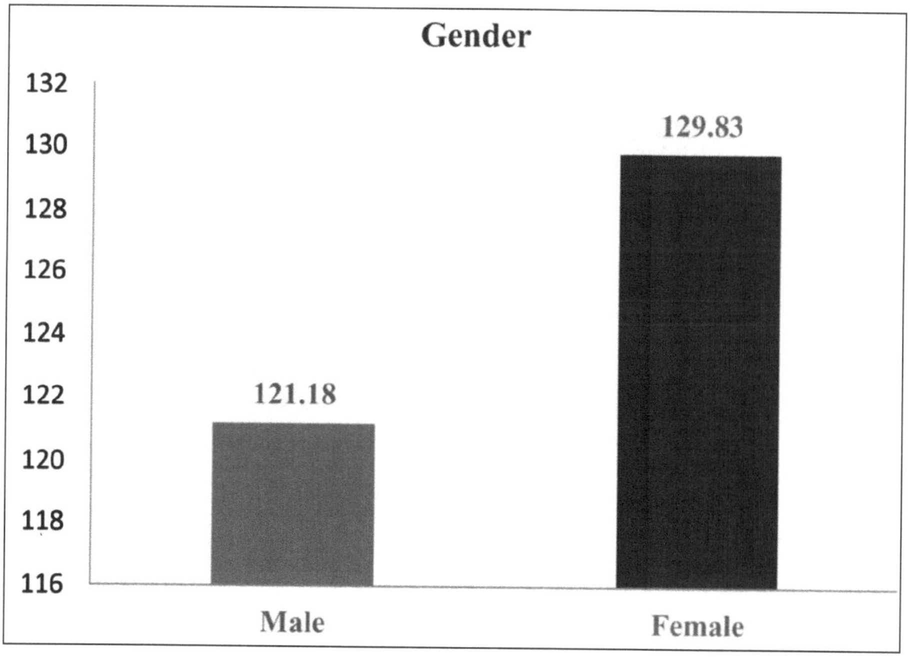

Fig. 4.7: Comparison of Mean between Boys & Girls of intermediate with respect their Emotional intelligence.

Table 4.6: Mean, SD. and t values for Academic stress of Intermediate Boys and Girls

S. No.	Gender	N	Mean	SD	't'-Value	df	Level of Significance
1.	Boys	572	127.33	15.07	12.95	1198	**
2.	Girls	628	119.57	18.84			

** - Significant at 0.01 level

It is evident from the above table that the computed value of t (12.95) is greater than the table/critical value of (2.58) at 0.01 level of significance. Hence, the Hypothesis is rejected for the variable gender. Hence, it is concluded that gender has significant influence on the Academic Stress of intermediate students.

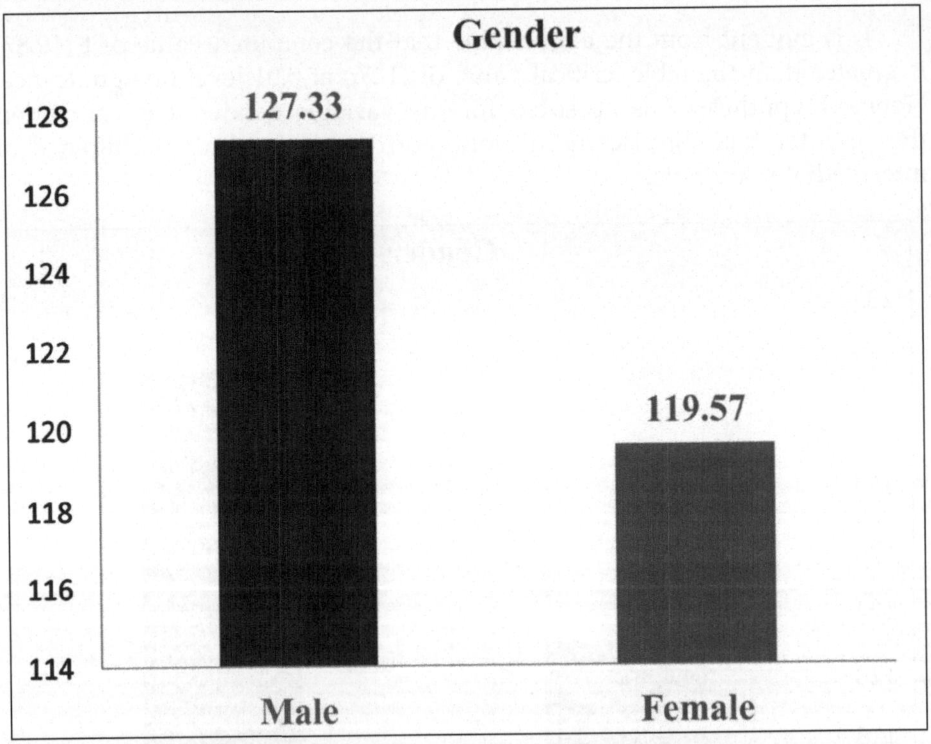

Fig. 4.8: Mean Comparison between Boys & Girls students with respect to Academic Stress

HYPOTHESIS-4

There would be no significant influence of management on emotional intelligence and academic stress of intermediate students.

In the present investigation the influence of management on emotional intelligence and academic stress of intermediate students is investigated. The corresponding emotional intelligence and academic stress scores of intermediate students studying in government and private colleges are analyzed accordingly. The influence of management on the emotional intelligence and academic stress is investigated using t -technique. The above hypothesis is tested by employing t technique. The results are presented in Tables 4.7 and 4.8 respectively.

Table 4.7: Mean, SD. and t values for Emotional Intelligence scores of Intermediate students for the variable Management

S. No.	Management	N	Mean	SD Value	't'-	df	Level of Significance
1.	Government	632	123.38	14.70	2.31	1198	*
2.	Private	568	125.64	14.16			

* - Significant at 0.05 level

From the above table it is clearly evident that computed value of t (2.31) is greater than the table/critical value (1.96) at 0.05 level of significance. Therefore, Hypothesis-4 is rejected for the variable management. Hence, it is concluded that management has significant influence on the emotional intelligence of intermediate students.

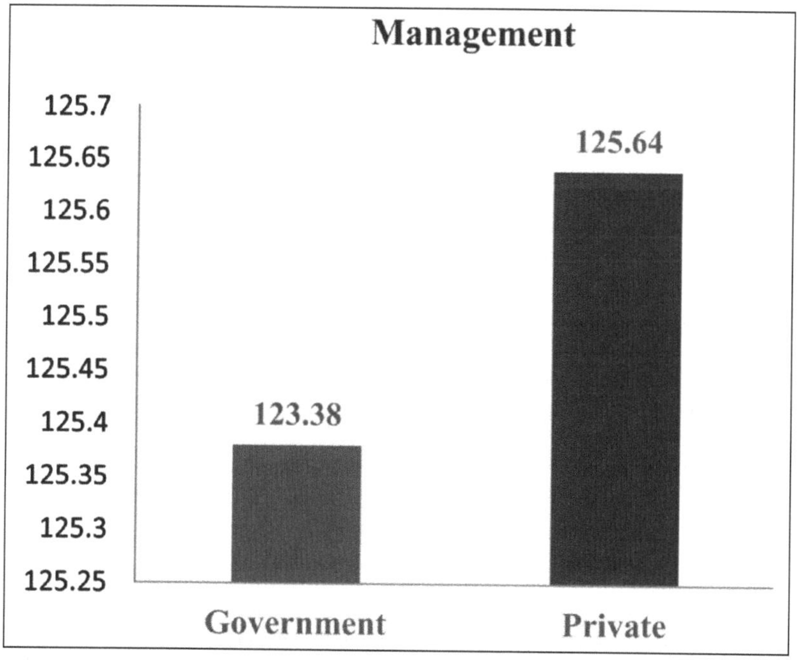

Fig. 4.9: Comparison of Means between Government and Private colleges of intermediate students with respect to Emotional intelligence

Table 4.8: Mean, SD and 't' values for the Academic Stress scores of Intermediate students for the variable Management

S. No.	Management	N	Mean	SD	't'-Value	df	Level of Significance
1.	Government	632	123.54	17.68	4.17	1198	**
2.	Private	568	123.36	18.56			

** - Significant at 0.01 level

From the above table it is evident that the computed value of t (4.17) is greater than the table/critical value (2.58) at 0.01 level of significant. Therefore, the above Hypothesis is rejected for the variable management and it is concluded that Government and Private College students differ significantly with regard to their Academic Stress. Intermediate students from private colleges are exhibiting more academic stress than government college students.

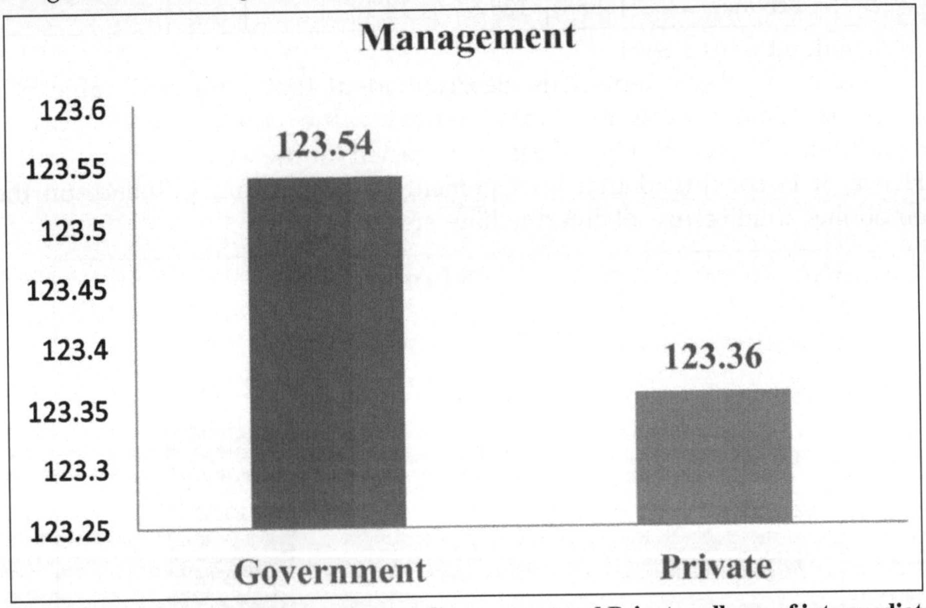

Fig. 4.10: Comparison of means between Government and Private colleges of intermediate students with respect to their Academic Stress

HYPOTHESIS-5

There would be no significant influence of locality on emotional intelligence and academic stress of intermediate students.

The influence of locality on the emotional intelligence and academic stress is investigated in the present study. The corresponding emotional intelligence scores of urban and rural intermediate students are analyzed accordingly. The influence of locality on the emotional intelligence and academic stress is investigated through t technique.

The above hypothesis is tested by employing t - technique. The results are presented in Table 4.9 and 4.10 respectively.

Table 4.9: Mean, SD and t value emotional intelligence scores of Rural and Urban Intermediate students

S. No.	Locality	N	Mean	SD	't'-Value	df	Level of Significance
1.	Rural	600	124.84	14.55	1.60	1198	@
2.	Urban	600	126.17	14.28			

@- Not Significant at 0.05 level

The table shows that the computed t value (1.60) is less than the table/critical value (1.96) at 0.05 level of significance. Hence, it is concluded that the formulated Hypothesis is true for the variable locality. Therefore locality does not have any significant influence on emotional intelligence of intermediate students.

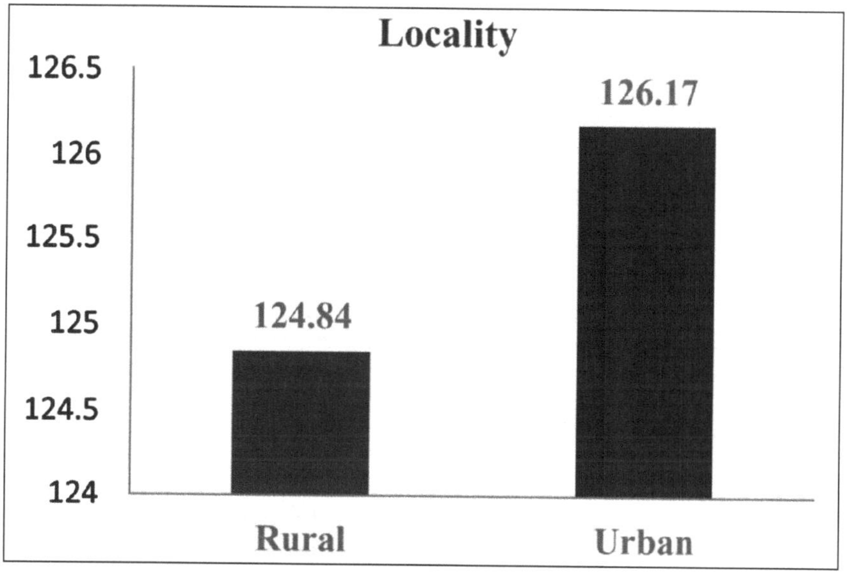

Fig. 4.11: Comparison of means between Rural & Urban intermediate students with reference to their Emotional intelligence

Table 4.10: Mean, SD and t values for academic stress scores of rural and urban intermediate students

S. No.	Locality	N	Mean	SD	't'-Value	df	Level of Significance
1.	Rural	600	124.84	14.55	0.85	1198	@
2.	Urban	600	126.17	14.28			

@- Significant at 0.05 level

It is clearly shown that the computed value of t (0.85) is less than the table/critical value (1.96) at 0.05 level of significance. Hence, the above Hypothesis is accepted and concluded that locality is not influencing significantly the Academic Stress of intermediate students. Both urban and rural intermediate students are exhibiting the same level of academic stress.

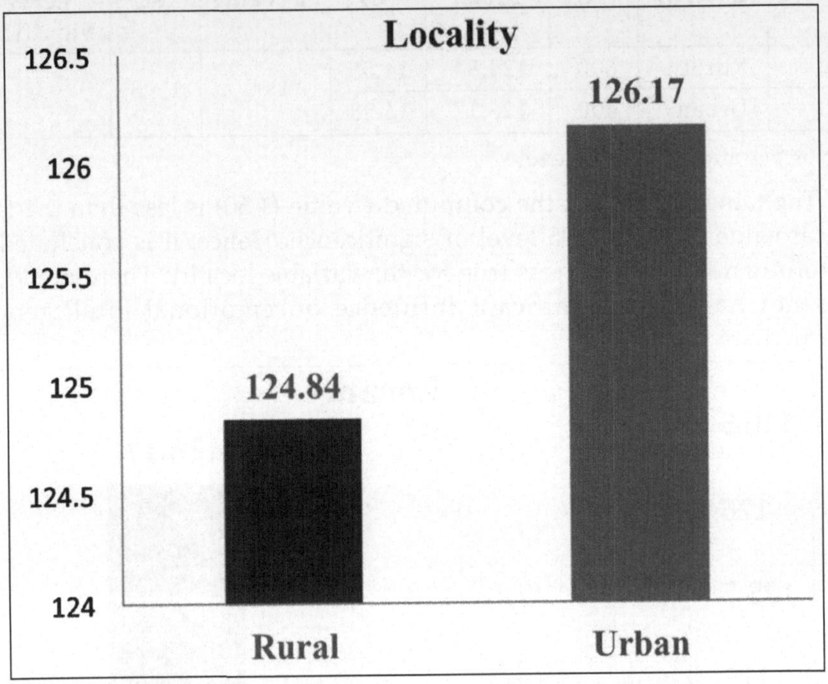

Fig. 4.12: Comparison of means between Rural and Urban intermediate students with respect to their Academic Stress

HYPOTHESIS-6

There would be no significant influence of nature of course on emotional intelligence and academic stress among intermediate students.

The influence of nature of course on emotional intelligence and academic stress of intermediate students is investigated in the present study. The corresponding emotional intelligence and academic stress scores of students studying in Arts and Science groups are analyzed accordingly. The influence of nature of course on emotional intelligence and academic stress are investigated through t -test.

The above hypothesis is tested by employing t - technique. The results are presented in Tables 4.11 and 4.12 respectively

Table 4.11: Mean, SD and t values for the emotional intelligence scores of Intermediate students with reference to their nature of course

S.No.	Nature of Course	N	Mean	SD	't'-Value	df	Level of Significance
1.	Arts	580	122.12	14.18	10.02	1198	**
2.	Science	620	130.25	13.40			

** - Significant at 0.01 level

It is evident from the above table that the calculated t value (10.02) is greater than the table value (1.96) at 0.01 level of significance. It shows that there is significant difference between intermediate students studying Arts and Science groups with reference to their emotional intelligence. Hence the formulated hypothesis is rejected for the variable nature of course. It is concluded that nature of course influences significantly emotional intelligence of Arts and Science group intermediate students.

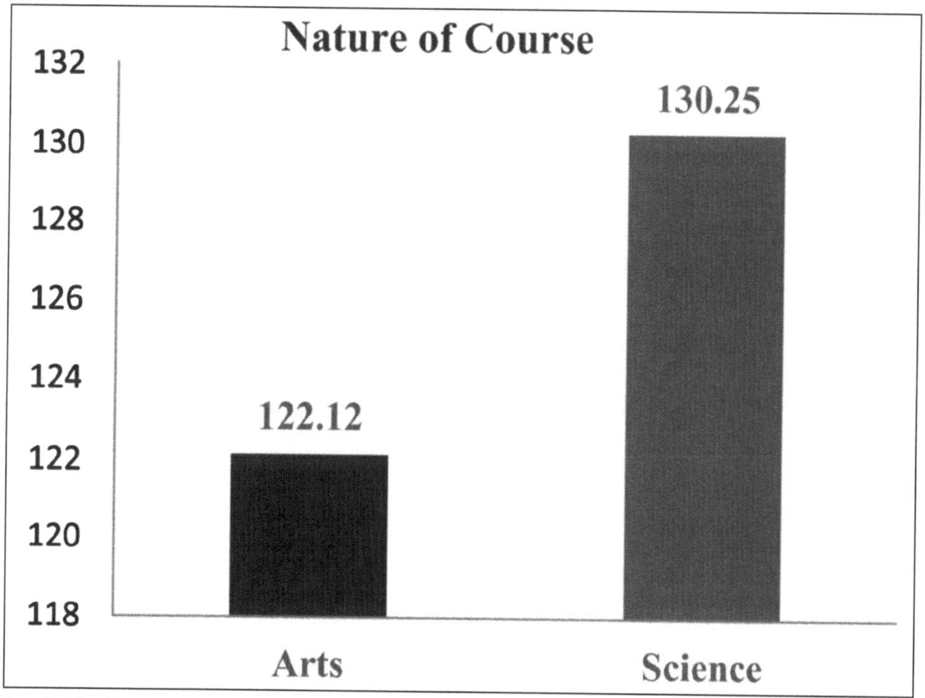

Fig. 4.13: Comparison of means between Arts & Science intermediate students with respect to their Emotional intelligence scores

Table 4.12: Mean, SD and t values for the Academic stress scores of Intermediate students with reference to their nature of course

S.No.	Nature of Course	N	Mean	SD	't'-Value	df	Level of Significance
1.	Arts	580	118.74	15.81	9.756**	1198	**
2.	Science	620	130.05	19.07			

** Significant at 0.01 level

It is clearly evident that the calculated 't value (9.756) is greater than the table/critical value of (2.58) at 0.01 level of significance and therefore, it can be concluded that there is significant difference between intermediate students studying from Arts and Science groups with reference to their academic stress. Hence this hypothesis is rejected and inferred that academic stress is an influencing factor with reference to nature of course.

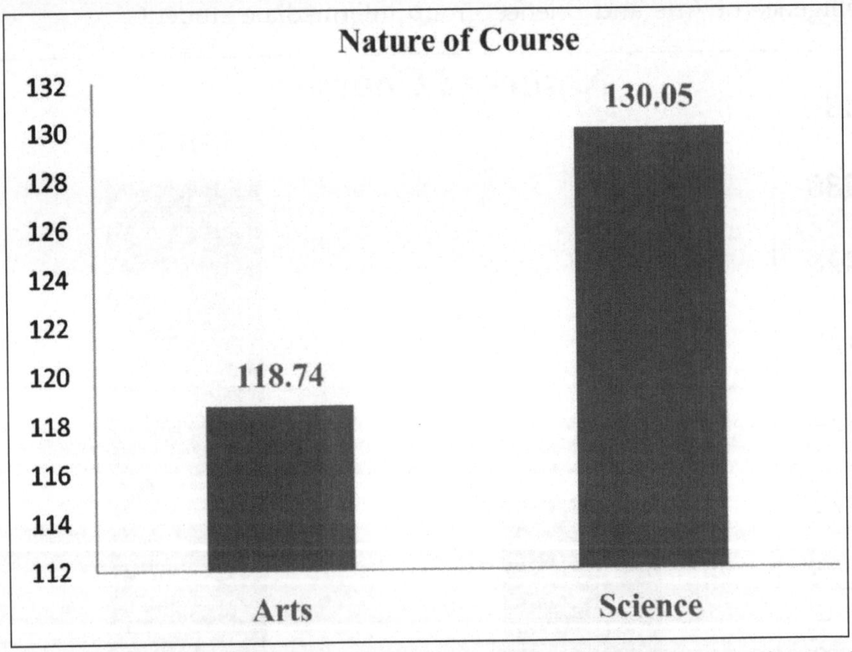

Fig. 4.14: Comparison of means between Arts and Science group intermediate students with respect to their Academic Stress scores

HYPOTHESIS-7

There would be no significant influence of medium of study on Emotional intelligence and academic stress of intermediate students.

In the present investigation the intermediate students are divided into two groups on the basis of medium: Telugu and English. The influence of medium on the emotional intelligence and academic stress is investigated.

The corresponding emotional intelligence and academic stress scores of English and Telugu medium students are analyzed accordingly. The influence of medium of study on the emotional intelligence and academic stress is investigated through t technique.

The above hypothesis is tested by employing t technique. The results are presented in Tables 4.13 and 4.14 respectively.

Table 4.13: Mean, SD and t value for emotional intelligence scores for the variable medium study

S.No.	Medium	N	Mean	SD	't'-Value	df	Level of Significance
1.	Telugu	550	121.28	14.20	8.85	1198	**
2.	English	650	128.53	13.83			

** - Significant at 0.01 level

It is evident from above table that the computed value of t (8.85) is greater than the table/critical value of (2.58) at 0.01 level of significant. Therefore, Hypothesis-7 is rejected for the variable medium study. Hence, it is concluded that medium of study has significant influence on the emotional intelligence of intermediate students.

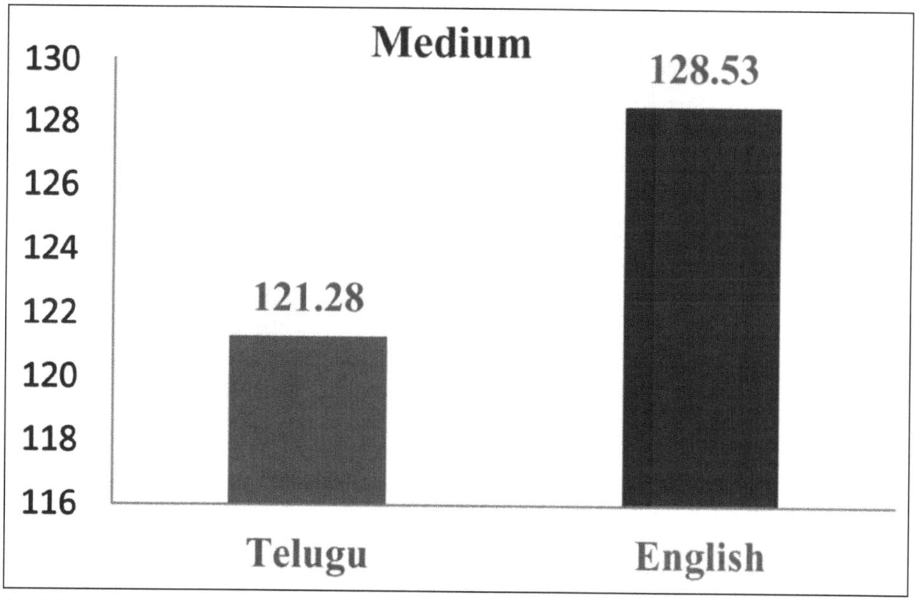

Fig. 4.15: Comparison of means between Telugu & English Medium intermediate students with respect to Emotional intelligence

Table 4.14: Mean, SD and t value for Academic Stress scores of the Intermediate students for the variable medium of study

S.No.	Medium	N	Mean	SD	't'-Value	df	Level of Significance
1.	Telugu	550	127.74	15.08	9.57	1198	**
2.	English	650	117.53	19.00			

** - Significant at 0.01 level

From above the table it is clearly evident that the computed value of t (9.57) is greater than the table/critical value of (2.58) at 0.01 level of significance. Hence, Hypothesis-7 is rejected for the variable medium of study and it is concluded that medium of study has significant influence on Academic Stress of intermediate students. From the mean values it can be interpreted that academic stress of intermediate students studying in English medium is much higher than the students studying in Telugu medium.

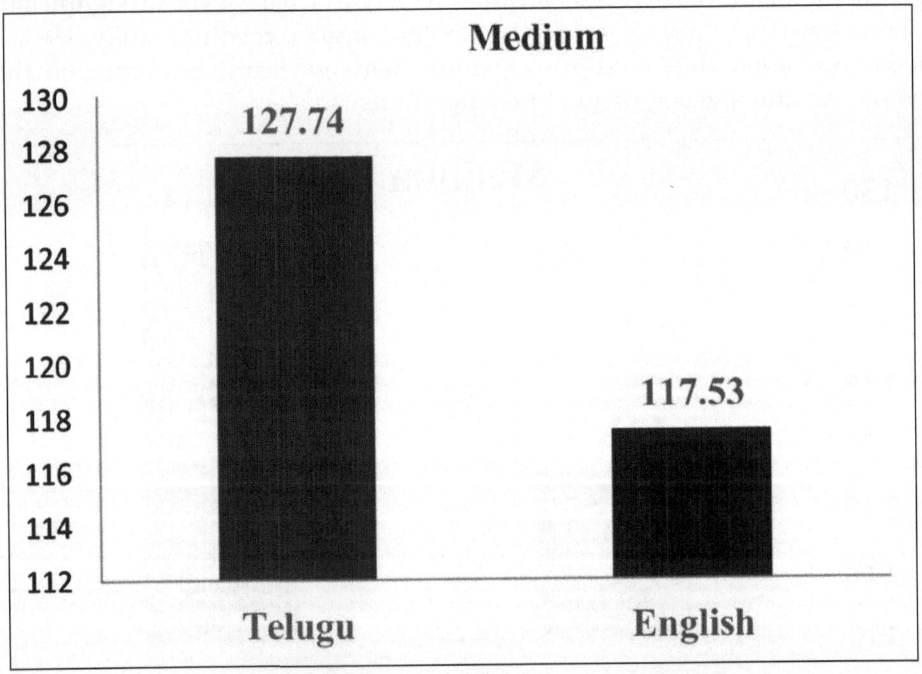

Fig. 4.16: Comparison of means between Telugu and English medium intermediate students with respect to their Academic Stress

HYPOTHESIS-8

There would be no significant influence of type of Residence on emotional intelligence and academic stress of intermediate students.

In the present study influence of type of Residence on emotional intelligence and academic stress of intermediate students is studied. The corresponding emotional intelligence and academic stress scores of Hostellers and Day scholars are analyzed accordingly. The influence of type of Residence on emotional intelligence and academic stress scores are observed by using t technique.

The above hypothesis is tested by employing t technique. The results are presented in Tables 4.15 and 4.16 respectively:

Table 4.15: Mean, SD and t values for emotional intelligence scores of Intermediate students for the variable type of Residence

Sl.No.	Type of Residence	N	Mean	SD	't'- Value	df	Level of Significance
1.	Hostlers	515	123.24	14.19	4.26	1198	**
2.	Day Scholars	685	131.27	13.94			

** - Significant at 0.01 level

It is clear from the above table that the calculated value of 't' (4.26) is greater than the table value (2.58) at 0.01 level of significance. The mean emotional intelligence scores of students residing in hostels is greater than the mean emotional intelligence scores of day scholar students. It can be interpreted that students residing in hostels are more emotionally intelligent than day scholar students. Hence the type of residence has significant influence on emotional intelligence of intermediate students.

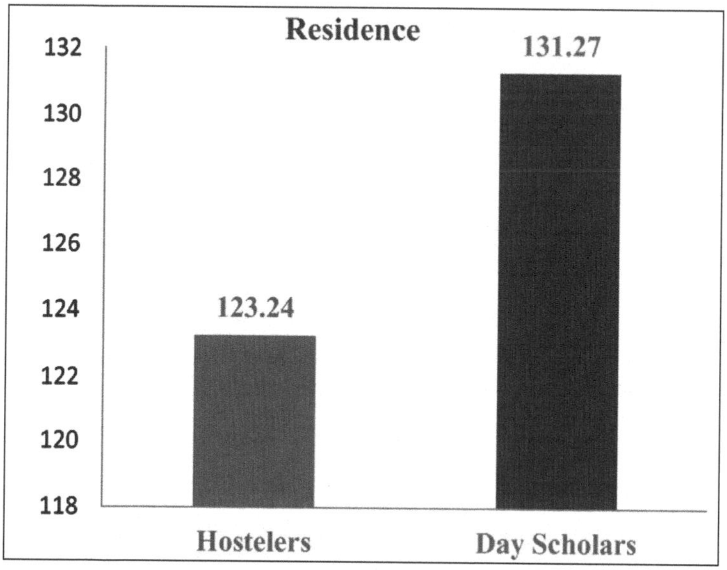

Fig. 4.17: Comparison of means between Hostlers and Day Scholars of intermediate students with respect to their Emotional intelligence

Table 4.16: Mean, SD and 't' values for the Academic Stress scores of the intermediate students for the variable type of Residence

Sl.No.	Type of Residence	N	Mean	SD	't'- Value	df	Level of Significance
1.	Hostlers	515	128.71	16.72	8.55	1198	**
2.	Day Scholars	685	120.38	16.66			

** - Significant at 0.01 level

It is clear from above table that the computed value of 't' (8.55) is greater than the table value (2.56) at 0.01 level of significance. Therefore, the formulated hypothesis is rejected for the variable type of Residence. It is concluded that type of Residence have significant influence on Academic Stress of intermediate students. It can be interpreted that students residing in hostels are having more academic stress than day scholar students

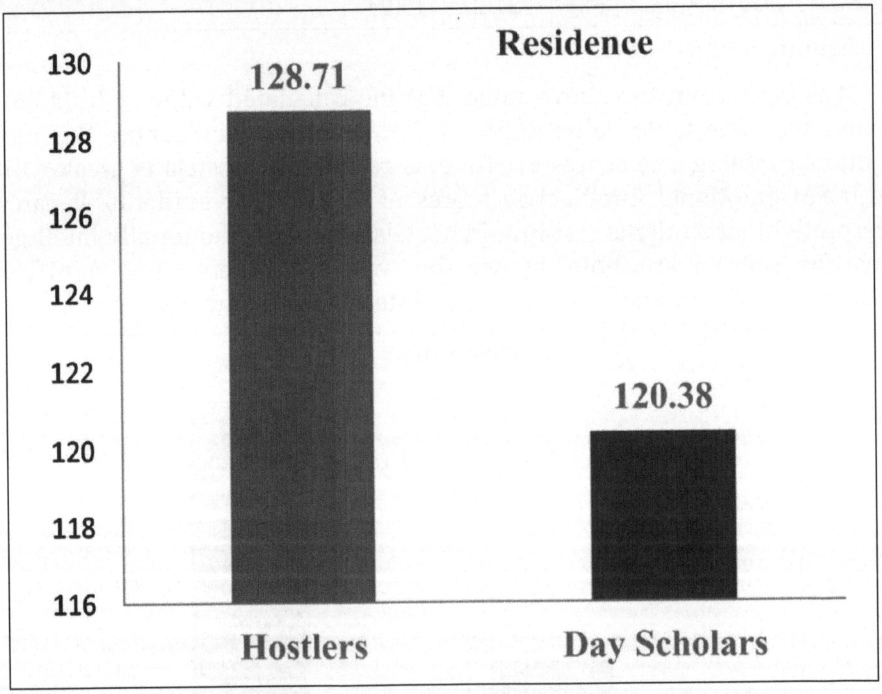

Fig. 4.18: Comparison of means between Hostlers and Day Scholars of intermediate students with respect to their Academic Stress

HYPOTHESIS-9

There would be no significant influence of Caste on Emotional intelligence and academic stress of intermediate students.

In the present investigation the selected sample of intermediate students are divided into four caste groups, SC, ST, BC and OC. The influence of Caste on the emotional intelligence and academic stress is investigated. The corresponding emotional intelligence and academic stress scores of four groups are analyzed accordingly. The influence of Caste on the emotional intelligence and academic stress is investigated through F values.

The above hypothesis is tested by employing F test. The results are presented in Tables 4.17 and 4.18 respectively.

Table-4.17(a): Mean, SD values for the emotional intelligence scores of intermediate students for the variable Caste

Sl. No.	Caste	N	Mean	SD
1.	SC	450	121.21	14.14
2.	ST	120	121.60	13.82
3.	BC	280	128.06	13.66
4.	OC	350	130.32	13.63

Table 4.17: (b): Analysis of variance (ANOVA) for emotional intelligence scores for the variable Caste

Source of Variance	Sum of Squares	df	Mean Square	F-Value	Level of Significance
Between Groups	20073.822	3	6691.274	14.20	**
Within Groups	229638.037	1196	192.005		
Total	249711.859	1199			

** - Significant at 0.01 level

It is clear from the above table that the computed value of F (14.20) is greater than the table value (6.64) for 3 and 1196 df at 0.01 level of significance. Therefore, Hypothesis is not accepted for the variable Caste. Hence, it is concluded that Caste has significant influence on emotional intelligence of intermediate students. From the mean values it can be concluded that OC and BC students are emotionally more intelligent than SC/ST students.

Table 4.18 (a): Mean, SD for the Academic Stress for the variable Caste

Sl. No.	Caste	N	Mean	Std. Deviation
1.	SC	450	127.50	14.99
2.	ST	120	132.14	15.51
3.	BC	280	126.70	18.22
4.	OC	350	120.34	19.50

Table 4.18 (b): Analysis of variance (ANOVA) for the Academic Stress for the variable Caste

Source of Variance	Sum of Squares	df	Mean Square	F-Value	Level of Significance
Between Groups	4705.488	3	1568.496	5.29	**
Within Groups	354910.345	1196	296.748		
Total	359615.833	1199			

** - Significant at 0.01 level

It is clear from table 4.18(b) that the computed value of F (5.29) is greater than the table value (3.78) for 3 and 1196 df at 0.01 level of significance. Therefore, Hypothesis-09 is not accepted for the variable Caste. Hence, it is concluded that Caste has significant influence on Academic Stress among intermediate students.

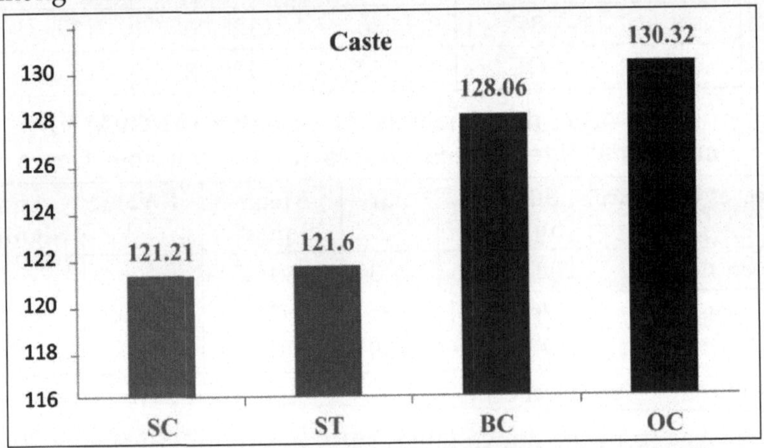

Fig. 4.19: Comparison of means between SC/ST, BC& OC community of intermediate students with respect to Emotional intelligence

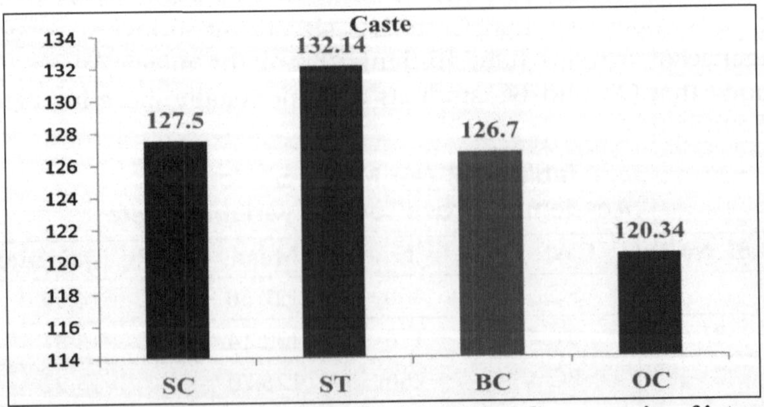

Fig. 4.20: Comparison of means between SC, ST, BC & OC community of intermediate students with respect to Academic Stress.

HYPOTHESIS-10

There would be no significant influence of Father's Education on emotional intelligence and academic stress of intermediate students.

In the present investigation the intermediate students are divided into four groups on the basis of Father's Education, Illiterate, Up to Intermediate, Graduation and Post Graduation or Professional Course. The influence of Father's Education on emotional intelligence and academic stress is investigated through F test.

The above hypothesis is tested by employing F technique. The results are presented in Tables 4.19 and 4.20 respectively.

Table 4.19 (a): Mean, SD for the emotional intelligence scores of intermediate students for the variable Father's Education.

Sl. No.	Father's Education	N	Mean	SD
1.	Illiterate	415	121.04	14.15
2.	Up to Intermediate	357	125.00	13.94
3.	Graduation	263	130.79	13.62
4.	Post Graduation or Professional Course	165	129.40	13.66

Table 4.19 (b): Analysis of variance (ANOVA) for emotional intelligence scores of intermediate students for the variable Father's Education

Source of Variance	Sum of Squares	df	Mean Square	F-Value	Level of Significance
Between Groups	18221.627	3	6073.876	31.38	**
Within Groups	231490.232	1196	193.554		
Total	249711.859	1199			

**- Significant at 0.01 level

It is clear from the above table that the computed value of F (31.38) is greater than the table value (6.64) for 3 and 1196 df at 0.01 level of significance. Therefore, Hypothesis is rejected for the variable Father's Education. It is concluded that Father's Education has significant influence on emotional intelligence of intermediate students.

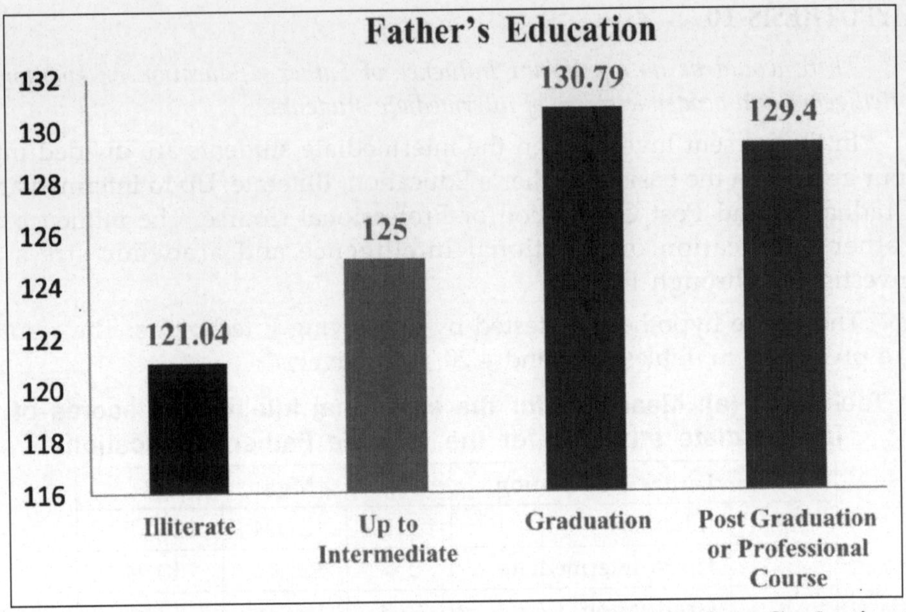

Fig. 4.21: Comparison of means between Illiterate, Up to Intermediate, Graduation & Post Graduation or Professional Course of father's education of intermediate students with respect to their Emotional intelligence

Table 4.20(a): Mean, SD for the Academic Stress scores of intermediate students for the variable Father's Education

Sl. No.	Father's Education	N	Mean	Std. Deviation
1.	Illiterate	415	132.34	15.03
2.	Up to Intermediate	357	122.43	17.18
3.	Graduation	263	120.86	17.89
4.	Post Graduation or Professional Course	165	120.23	21.45

Table 4.20(b): Analysis of variance (ANOVA) for Academic Stress for the variable Father's Education

Source of Variance	Sum of Squares	df	Mean Square	F-Value	Level of Significance
Between Groups	5830.281	3	1943.427	6.49	**
Within Groups	357985.552	1196	299.319		
Total	363815.833	1199			

**- Significant at 0.01 level

It is clear from table that the computed value of F (6.49) is greater than the table value (3.78) for 3 and 1196 df at 0.01 level of significance.

Therefore, Hypothesis is rejected for the variable Father's Education. Hence, it is concluded that Father's Education has significant influence on Academic Stress among intermediate students.

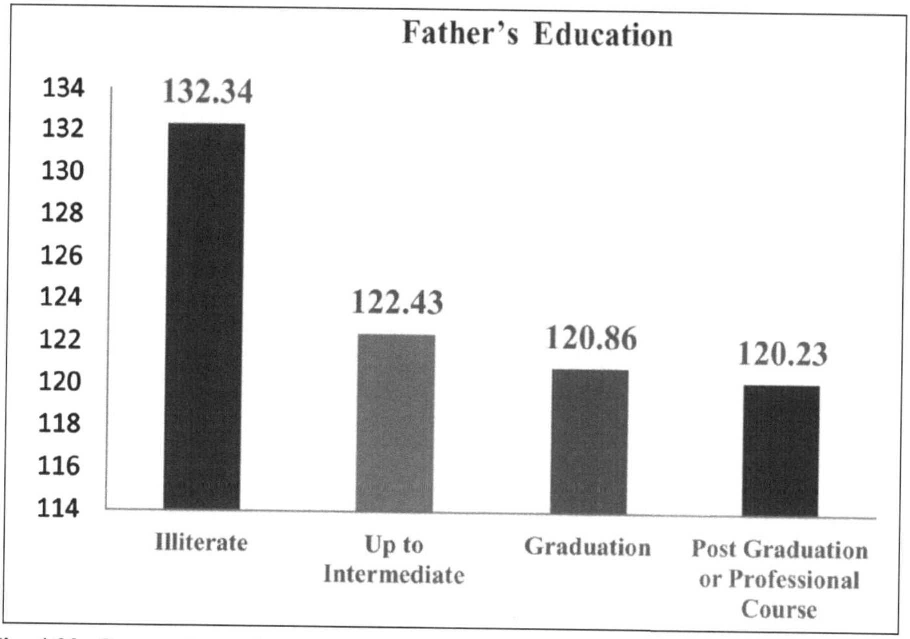

Fig. 4.22: Comparison of means between Illiterate, Up to Intermediate, Graduation & Post Graduation or Professional Course of father's education of intermediate students with respect to Academic Stress

HYPOTHESIS-11

There would be no significant influence of Mother's Education on Emotional intelligence and academic stress of intermediate students.

In the present investigation the selected sample of intermediate students are classified into four groups on the basis of their Mother's Education, Illiterate mothers, Up to Intermediate mothers, Graduation mothers and Post-Graduation or Professional Mothers. The influence of Mother's Education on the emotional intelligence and academic stress of intermediate students is investigated through F test.

The above hypothesis is tested by employing F technique. The results are presented in Tables 4.21 and 4.22 respectively:

Table 4.21 (a): Mean, SD for emotional intelligence of intermediate students for the variable Mother's Education

Sl. No.	Mother's Education	N	Mean	SD
1.	Illiterate	480	121.02	14.17
2.	Up to Intermediate	265	125.46	13.82
3.	Graduation	353	128.15	13.35
4.	Post Graduation or Professional Course	102	130.88	13.980

Table 4.21(b): Analysis of variance (ANOVA) for the emotional intelligence of intermediate students for the variable Mother's Education

Source of Variance	Sum of Squares	df	Mean Square	F-Value	Level of Significance
Between Groups	20604.052	3	6868.017	35.85	**
Within Groups	229107.807	1196	191.562		
Total	249711.859	1199			

** - Significant at 0.01 level

It is clear from the above table that the computed value of F (35.85) is greater than the table value (3.78) for 3 and 1196 df at 0.01 level of significance. Therefore, the formulated Hypothesis is not accepted for the variable Mother's Education. Hence it is concluded that Mother's Education has significant influence on emotional intelligence of intermediate students.

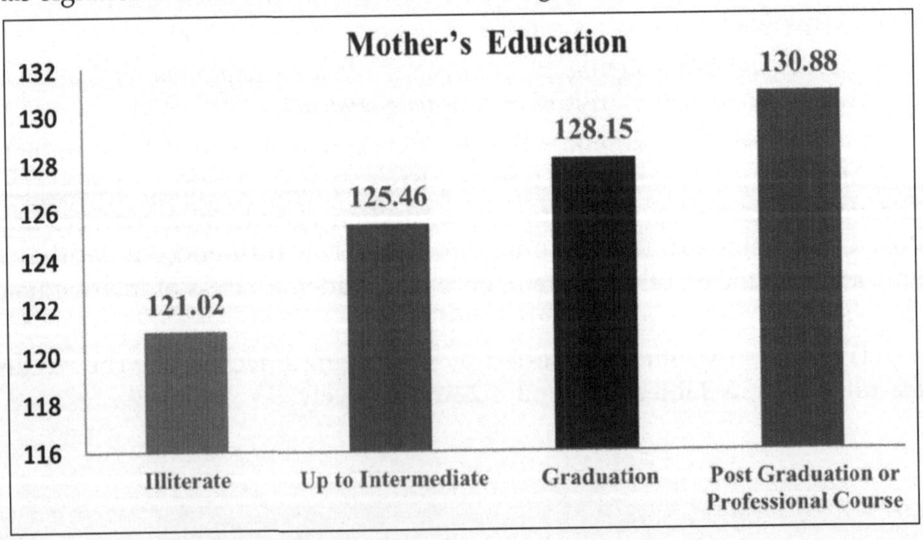

Fig. 4.23: Comparison of means for emotional intelligence of intermediate students with reference to their mothers' education

Table 4.22(a): Mean, SD for Academic Stress of intermediate students for the variable Mother's Education

Sl. No.	Mother's Education	N	Mean	SD
1.	Illiterate	480	133.49	15.02
2.	Up to Intermediate	265	130.42	17.10
3.	Graduation	353	121.65	18.48
4.	Post Graduation or Professional Course	102	115.83	21.46

Table 4.22(b): Analysis of variance (ANOVA) for the Academic Stress of intermediate students for the variable Mother's Education

Source of Variance	Sum of Squares	df	Mean Square	F-Value	Level of Significance
Between Groups	8608.862	3	2869.621	9.75	**
Within Groups	352206.970	1196	294.487		
Total	360815.832	1199			

** - Significant at 0.01 level

It is clear from the above table that the computed value of F (9.75) is greater than the table value (3.78) for 3 and 1196 df at 0.01 level of significance. Therefore, the above Hypothesis is not accepted for the variable Mother's Education at 0.01 level of significance. Hence it is concluded that Mother's Education has significant influence on Academic Stress among intermediate students.

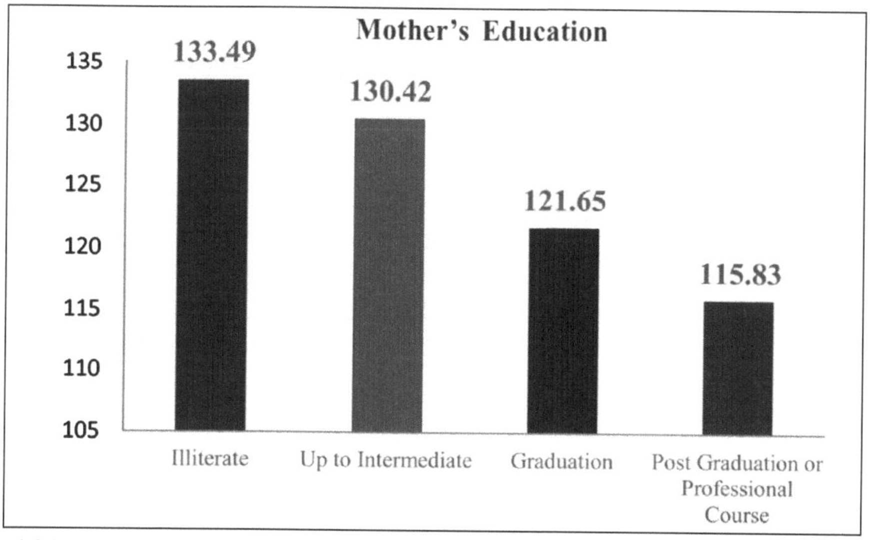

Fig. 4.24: Comparison of means for Academic Stress of intermediate students with reference to their mothers education

HYPOTHESIS-12

There would be no significant influence of Father's Occupation on Emotional intelligence and academic stress of intermediate students.

In the present investigation the selected sample of intermediate students are classified into four groups on the basis of their Father's occupation Labor, Agriculture, Business and Employee. The influence of Father's occupation on the emotional intelligence and academic stress of intermediate students is investigated through F test.

The above hypothesis is tested by employing F - technique. The results are presented in Tables 4.23 and 4.24 respectively.

Table 4.23 (a): Mean, SD for the emotional intelligence scores of intermediate students for their Father's Occupation

Sl. No.	Father's Occupation	N	Mean	SD
1.	Labor	415	120.23	13.84
2.	Agriculture	358	125.03	14.18
3.	Business	262	130.81	13.31
4.	Employee	165	129.10	14.02

Table 4.23 (b): Analysis of variance (ANOVA) for emotional intelligence of intermediate students for the variable Father's Occupation

Source of Variance	Sum of Squares	df	Mean Square	F-Value	Level of Significance
Between Groups	20052.927	3	6684.309	9.60	**
Within Groups	229658.932	1196	192.023		
Total	249711.859	1199			

**- Significant at 0.01 level

It is evident from the above table that the computed value of F (9.60) is greater than the table value (3.78) for 3 and 1196 df at 0.01 level of significance. Therefore, Hypothesis is rejected for the variable Father's Occupation. Hence, it is concluded that Father's Occupation has significant influence on emotional intelligence of intermediate students. It can be interpreted from the mean values that emotional intelligence of intermediate students whose fathers occupation are employees and business persons is higher than that of students whose fathers are in labor work and agriculture work.

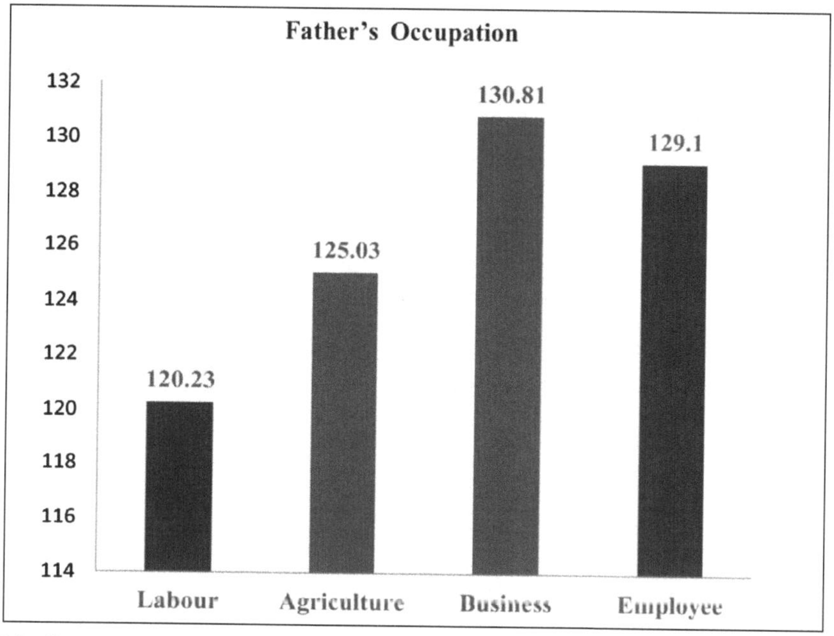

Fig. 4.25: Comparison of means for Emotional intelligence of intermediate students with reference to their Father's occupation

Table 4.24(a): Mean, SD for the Academic Stress scores of intermediate students for their Father's Occupation

Sl. No.	Father's Occupation	N	Mean	SD
1.	Labour	415	134.15	17.04
2.	Agriculture	358	131.48	18.03
3.	Business	262	127.62	21.53
4.	Employee	165	123.45	18.12

Table 4.24(b): Analysis of variance (ANOVA) for Academic Stress for the variable Father's Occupation

Source of Variance	Sum of Squares	df	Mean Square	F-Value	Level of Significance
Between Groups	8980.590	3	2993.530	10.00	**
Within Groups	357835.241	1196	299.193		
Total	366815.831	1199			

**- Significant at 0.01 level

It is clear from the above table that the computed value of F (10.00) is greater than the table value (3.78) for 3 and 1196 df at 0.01 level of significance. Therefore, Hypothesis-29 is rejected for the variable Father's

Occupation. Hence, it is concluded that Father's Occupation has significant influence on Academic Stress among intermediate students. It can be concluded from the mean values that the academic stress of intermediate students whose fathers are in agriculture work and labour work are pruned to more academic stress than the students whose fathers are employed and business people.

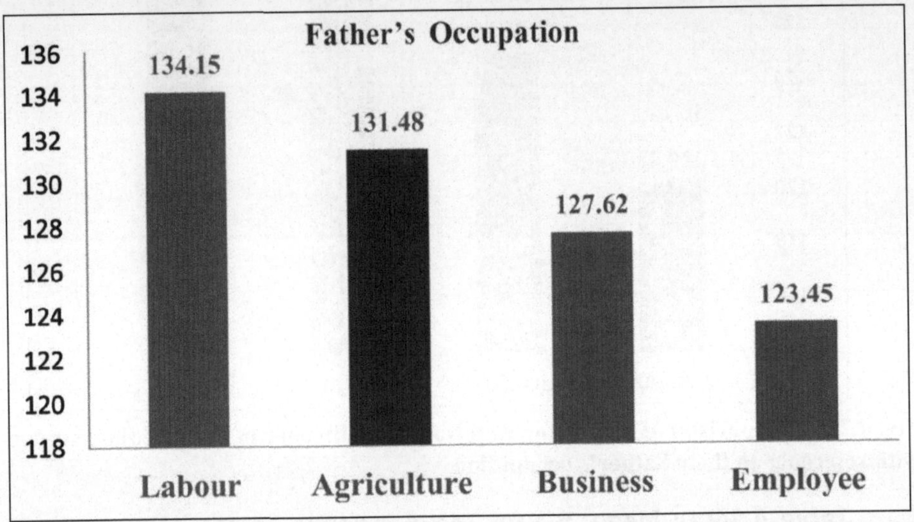

Fig. 4.26: Comparison of means for Academic Stress of intermediate students with reference to their Father's occupation

HYPOTHESIS-13

There would be no significant influence of Mother's Occupation on emotional intelligence and academic stress of intermediate students.

In the present investigation the intermediate students are classified into five groups. On the basis of Mother's Occupation, House Wife, Labour, Agriculture, Business and Employee. The influence of Mother's Occupation on the emotional intelligence and academic stress is investigated through F technique. The above hypothesis is tested by employing F technique. The results are presented in Tables 4.25 and 4.26 respectively:

Table 4.25 (a): Mean, SD for the emotional intelligence scores of intermediate students for the variable Mother's Occupation

Sl. No.	Mother's Occupation	N	Mean	SD
1.	House wife	323	119.70	13.86
2.	Labour	357	124.28	14.15
3.	Agriculture	230	129.95	13.30
4.	Business	168	130.78	13.61
5.	Employee	122	128.81	13.80

Table 4.25(b): Analysis of variance (ANOVA) for emotional intelligence for the variable Mother's Occupation

Source of Variance	Sum of Squares	df	Mean	F-Value Square	Level of Significance
Between Groups	1004.724	4	251.181	1.31	@
Within Groups	227747.134	1195	190.583		
Total	248751.858	1199			

@ - Significant at 0.05 level

It is clear from the above table the calculated value of F (1.31) is less than the table value (2.37) for 4 and 1195 df at 0.05 level of significance. Therefore, the above hypothesis is accepted for the variable Mother's Occupation. Hence it is concluded that Mother's Occupation does not have any significant influence on emotional intelligence of intermediate students. It can be inferred that emotional intelligence of intermediate students are similar with reference to their mothers occupation.

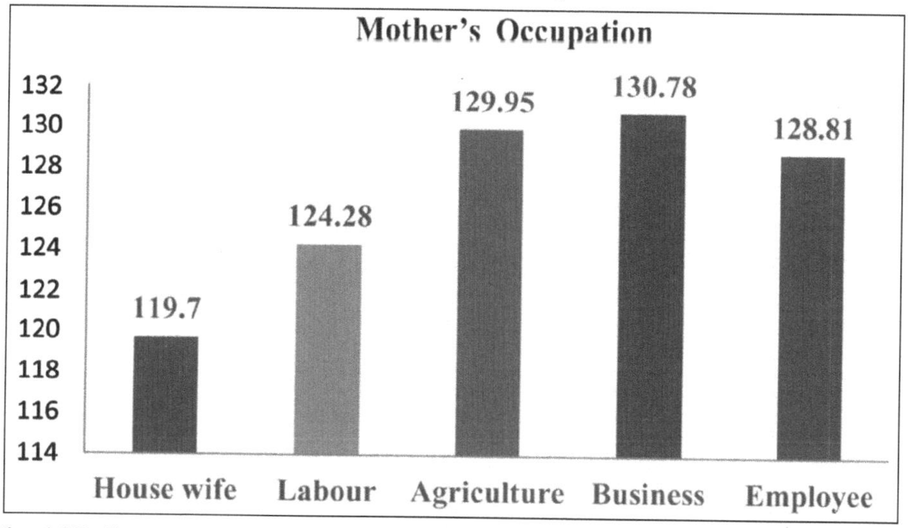

Fig. 4.27: Comparison of means for Emotional intelligence of intermediate students with reference to their mother's occupation

Table 4.26(a): Mean, SD for the Academic Stress scores of intermediate students for the variable Mother's Occupation

Sl. No.	Mother's Occupation	N	Mean	SD
1.	House wife	323	129.92	14.80
2.	Labour	357	133.04	16.53
3.	Agriculture	230	127.68	17.57
4.	Business	168	123.34	18.69
5.	Employee	122	120.13	21.66

Table 4.26(b): Analysis of variance (ANOVA) for Academic Stress for the variable Mother's Occupation

Source of Variance	Sum of Squares	df	Mean Square	F-Value	Level of Significance
Between Groups	39987.238	4	9996.810	3.37	**
Within Groups	353828.594	1195	296.091		
Total	393815.833	1199			

** - Significant at 0.01 level

It is clear from table that the computed value of F (3.37) is greater than the table value (3.32) for 4 and 1195 df at 0.01 level of significance. Therefore, Hypothesis is not accepted for the variable Mother's Occupation. Hence, it is concluded that Mother's Occupation has significant influence on Academic Stress among intermediate students. It can be inferred that academic stress of intermediate students whose mothers occupation is agriculture, labour, house holder is higher than that of students whose mothers of employees and business personals.

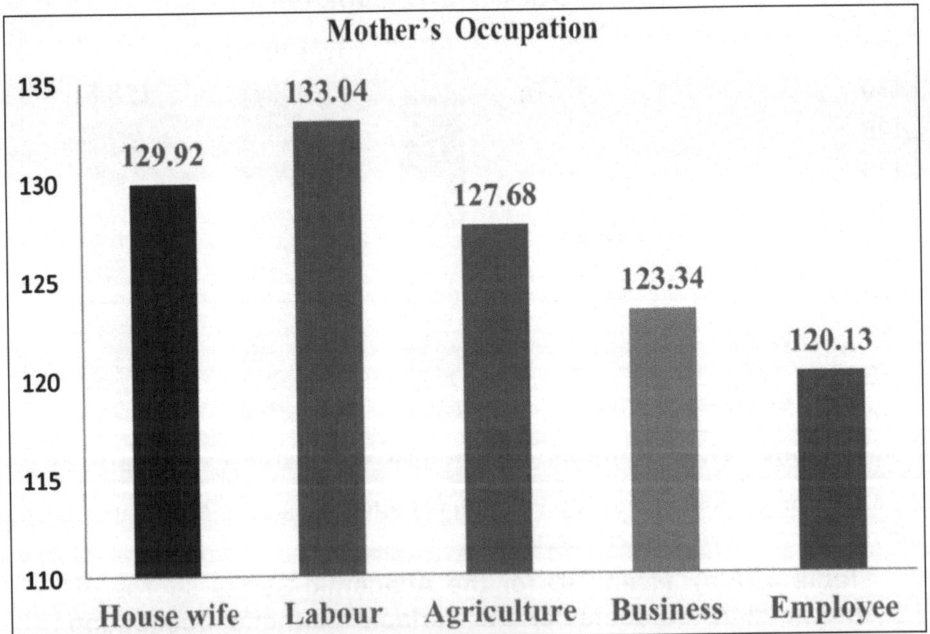

Fig. 4.28: Comparison of means for Academic Stress of intermediate students with reference to their mother's occupation

HYPOTHESIS-14

There would be no significant influence of Annual Income of Family on Emotional intelligence and academic stress of intermediate students.

In the present investigation the intermediate students are divided into three groups on the basis of Annual Income of their Family, Below Rs: One Lakh, Between Rs: One lakh to – Two lakhs, and Above Rs: Two lakhs. The influence of Annual Income of the Family on the emotional intelligence and academic stress of intermediate students is investigated through F - technique.

The above hypothesis is tested by employing F technique. The results are presented in Tables 4.27 and 4.28 respectively.

Table 4.27(a): Mean, SD for the of emotional intelligence scores of intermediate students for the variable Annual Income of their Family

Sl. No.	Annual Income of the Family	N	Mean	SD
1.	Below 1 Lakh	505	121.31	14.17
2.	Between 1 lakh – 2 lakhs	435	128.04	13.85
3.	Above 2 lakhs	260	129.42	13.81

Table 4.27(b): Analysis of variance (ANOVA) fo emotional intelligence of intermediate students for the variable Annual Income of their Family

Source of Variance	Sum of Squares	df	Mean Square	F-Value	Level of Significance
Between Groups	1047.836	2	523.918	2.67	@
Within Groups	234064.024	1197	195.542		
Total	235111.900	1199			

@ - Not Significant at 0.05 level

It is clear from table that the computed value of F (2.67) is less than the table value (2.99) for 2 and 1197 df at 0.05 level of not significance. Therefore, Hypothesis is accepted for the variable Annual Income of the Family at 0.05 level of significance. Hence, it is concluded that Annual Income of the Family does not have any significant influence on emotional intelligence of intermediate students.

Table 4.28(a): Mean, SD for Academic Stress scores of intermediate students for the variable Annual Income of the Family

Sl. No.	Annual Income of the Family	N	Mean	SD
1.	Below 1 Lakh	505	132.78	15.03
2.	Between 1 lakh – 2 lakhs	435	126.50	18.37
3.	Above 2 lakhs	260	119.37	20.02

Table 4.28(b): Analysis of variance (ANOVA) for Academic Stress scores of intermediate students for the variable Annual Income of the Family

Source of Variance	Sum of Squares	df	Mean Square	F-Value	Level of Significance
Between Groups	9371.693	2	4685.846	15.39	**
Within Groups	364444.140	1197	304.465		
Total	373815.833	1199			

** - Significant at 0.01 level

It is clear from table that the calculated value of F (15.39) is greater than the table value (4.66) for 2 and 1197 df at 0.05 level of significance. Therefore, the above hypothesis is not accepted for the variable Annual Income of the Family. Hence, it is concluded that Annual Income of the Family has significant influence on Academic Stress of intermediate students. It is inferred that lower the income of family, higher is the level of academic stress of students.

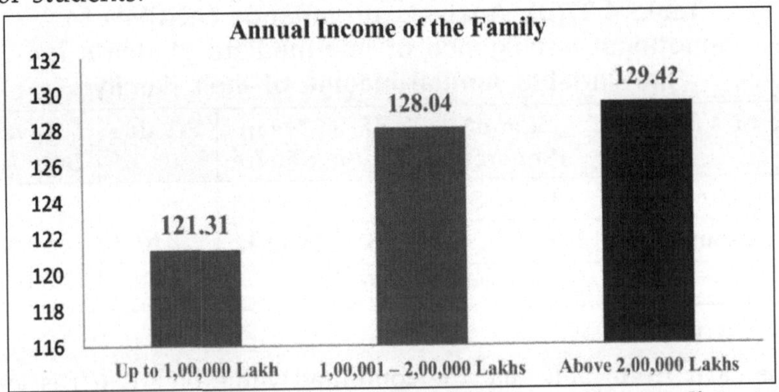

Fig. 4.29: Comparison of means for Emotional intelligence of intermediate students of their family income

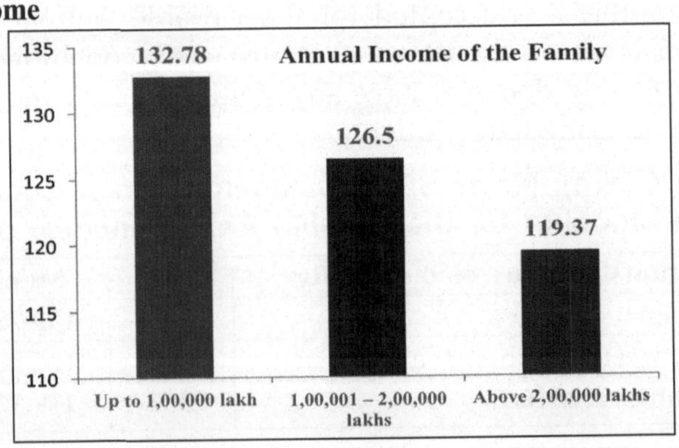

Fig. 4.30: Comparison of means of Academic Stress of intermediate students for their Annual Income of the Family

HYPOTHESIS-15

There would be no significant influence of Number of Members in the Family on Emotional intelligence and academic stress of intermediate students.

In the present investigation the intermediate students are divided into three groups: On the basis of Number of Members in the Family, Less than-3, 4-6 and above 6 members. The influence of Size of the Family on emotional intelligence and academic stress is investigated through F technique.

The above hypothesis is tested by employing F technique. The results are presented in Tables 4.29 and 4.30 respectively.

Table 4.29(a): Mean, SD for the emotional intelligence scores of intermediate students for the variable Size of the Family

Sl. No.	Size of the Family	N	Mean	SD
1.	Up – 3 members	555	121.35	14.10
2.	4 – 6 members	455	128.95	13.73
3.	Above 6 members	190	127.41	13.78

Table 4.29(b): Analysis of variance (ANOVA) for the emotional intelligence of intermediate students for the variable Size of the Family

Source of Variance	Sum of Squares	df	Mean Square	F-Value	Level of Significance
Between Groups	460.876	2	230.438	1.19	@
Within Groups	231850.983	1197	193.693		
Total	232311.859	1199			

@ - Not Significant at 0.05 level

It is clear from the above table that the computed value of F (1.19) is less than the table value (2.99) for 2 and 1197 df at 0.05 level of significance. Therefore the Hypothesis is accepted for the variable Size of the Family at 0.05 level of significance. Hence, it is concluded that Size of the Family does not have any significant influence on Emotional intelligence of intermediate students.

Table 4.30(a): Mean, SD for the Academic Stress of intermediate students for the variable Size of the Family

Sl. No.	Size of the Family	N	Mean	SD
1.	Up – 3 members	555	117.71	15.08
2.	4 – 6 members	455	128.26	18.33
3.	Above 6 members	190	128.71	20.77

Table 4.30(b): Analysis of variance (ANOVA) for the Academic Stress of intermediate students for the variable Size of the Family

Source of Variance	Sum of Squares	df	Mean Square	F-Value	Level of Significance
Between Groups	34072.855	2	2036.427	6.78	**
Within Groups	359742.978	1197	300.537		
Total	393815.833	1199			

Note: ** - Significant at 0.01 level

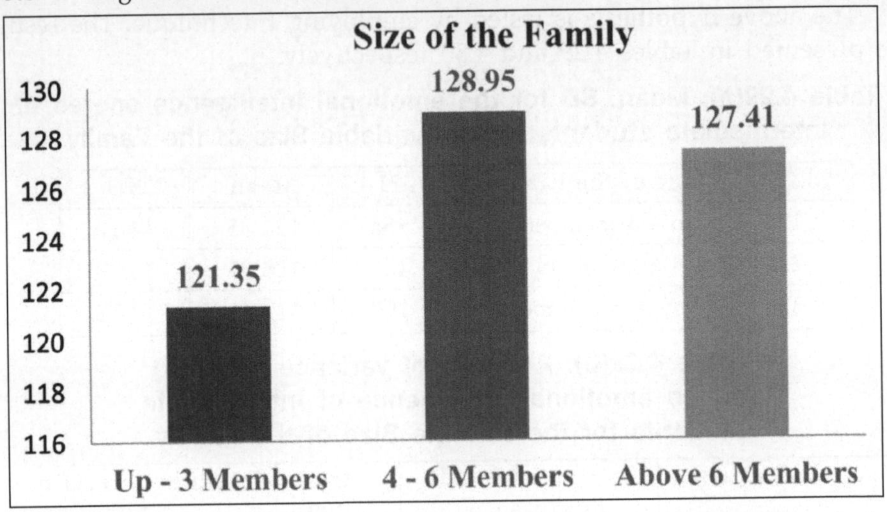

Fig. 4.31: Comparison of means for emotional intelligence of intermediate students with reference to size of family

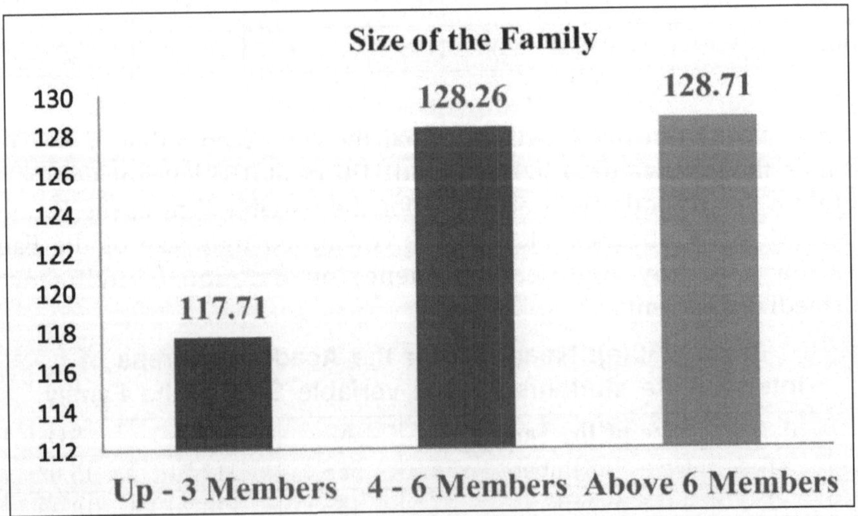

Fig. 4.32: Comparison of means for academic stress of intermediate students with reference to size of family

It is clear from table 4.30 that the computed value of F (6.78) is greater than the table value (4.66) for 2 and 1197 df at 0.01 level of significance. Therefore, Hypothesis is not accepted for the variable Size of the Family. Hence, it is concluded that Size of the Family has significant influence on Academic Stress among intermediate students. It is inferred that increase in number of family members, higher is the academic stress of intermediate stress.

HYPOTHESIS-16

There would be no significant influence of Type of the Family on Emotional intelligence and academic stress of intermediate students.

In the present investigation the intermediate students are sub divided into two groups on the basis of Type of the Family as Joint Family and Nuclear family. The influence of type of family on emotional intelligence and academic stress is investigated. The corresponding emotional intelligence and academic stress scores of two groups are analyzed accordingly. The influence of type of family on emotional intelligence and academic stress of intermediate students is investigated through t -test.

The above hypothesis is tested by employing t - technique. The results are presented in Tables 4.31 and 4.32 respectively.

Table 4.31: Mean, SD and t value for emotional intelligence scores for the variable type of family

S.No.	Type of the Family	N	Mean	SD	't'-Value	df	Level of Significance
1.	Joint Family	445	121.29	14.15	5.76	1198	**
2.	Nuclear	745	128.08	13.99			

Note: **- Significant at 0.01 level

It is evident from the above table that the computed value of t (5.76) is greater than the table/critical value of (2.58) at 0.01 level of significance. Therefore, the above hypothesis is rejected for the variable type of the family. Hence, it is concluded that type of the family has significant influence on Emotional intelligence of intermediate students. It can be inferred that there is a significant difference in the emotional intelligence of intermediate students belonging to nuclear family and joint families, students from joint families are emotionally more intelligent than from nuclear families.

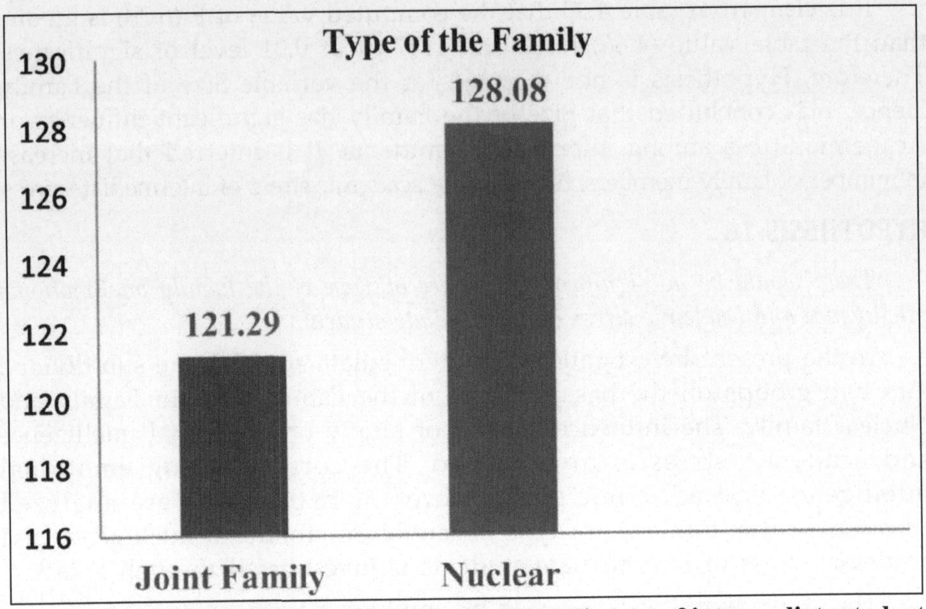

Fig. 4.33: Comparison of means for emotional intelligence of intermediate students with reference to their type of Family

Table 4.32: Mean, SD and t value of Academic Stress score of intermediate students for the variable Type of the Family

S. No.	Type of the Family	N	Mean	SD	't'-Value	df	Level of Significance
1.	Joint Family	455	127.03	15.01	2.25	1198	*
2.	Nuclear	745	117.60	18.92			

@ - Not Significant at 0.05 level

It is evident from table that the computed value of t (2.25) is greater than the table/critical value of (1.96) at 0.05 level of significant. Therefore, Hypothesis is accepted for the variable Type of the Family. Hence, it is concluded that Type of the Family has significant influence on the Academic Stress of intermediate students. It is clear that academic stress of intermediate students belonging to joint families is higher than the academic stress of intermediate students belonging to nuclear families.

PEARSONS CO-EFFICIENT CORRELATION BETWEEN EMOTIONAL INTELLIGENCE AND ACADEMIC STRESS

HYPOTHESIS-17

There would be no significant relationship between emotional intelligence and academic stress of intermediate students.

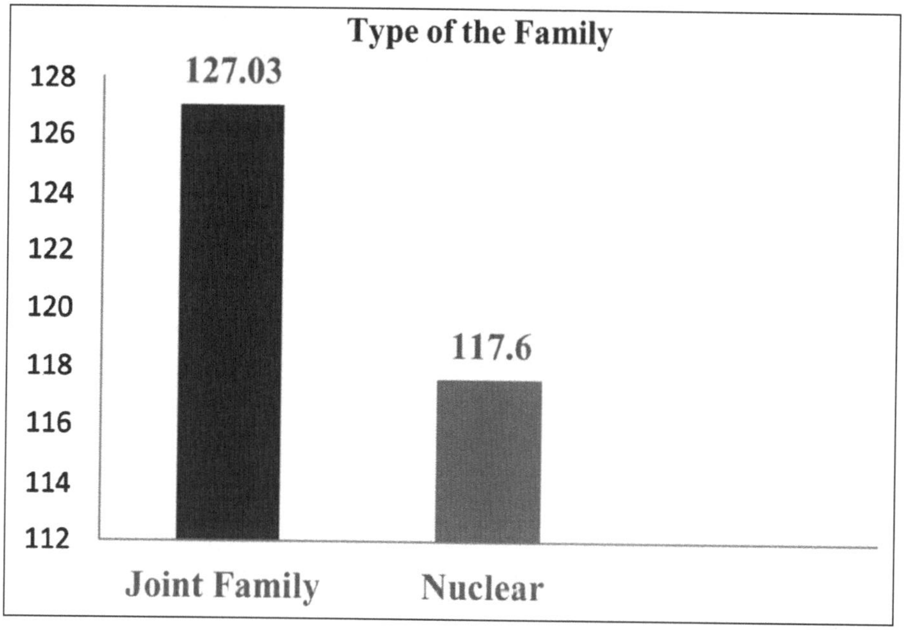

Fig. 4.34: Comparison of means for Academic Stress of intermediate students with reference to their type of Family

In the present study an attempt is made to find out whether there is any significant relationship between emotional intelligence and academic stress among selected sample groups of intermediate students. According to this the hypothesis is formulated and tested for co-efficient of correlation using Pearson's product moment method.

Table 4.33: Shows relationship between emotional intelligence and academic stress among intermediate students

Variables	r - Value
Emotional Intelligence and Academic Stress	-0.427 **

Table 4.34 shows that there was significant negative relationship between emotional intelligence and academic stress among intermediate students. Hence, the hypothesis is rejected on concluded that higher the emotional intelligence of the students lower is the academic stress.

HYPOTHESIS-18

There would be no significance difference in the levels of emotional intelligence of intermediate students with respect to the variables gender, locality and type of management.

Table 4.34: Levels of Emotional Intelligence based on Gender

Levels of Emotional Intelligence		Gender		F-Value
		Boys	Girls	
Low	Mean	108.63	110.73	20.06 **
	SD	6.80	5.35	
Moderate	Mean	126.80	128.55	
	SD	4.58	4.93	
High	Mean	144.43	142.71	
	SD	5.45	6.10	

**-Significant at 0.01 level

The above table gives the mean scores for emotional intelligence of boys and girls studying intermediate. The obtained F value 20.06 reveals that there is significant mean difference between boys and girls with reference to the levels of emotional intelligence. From the mean values can be concluded that girls are better than boys at low and moderate levels of emotional intelligence. At the high level of emotional intelligence, boys are better than girls.

Table 4.35: Levels of Emotional Intelligence based on Locality

Levels of Emotional Intelligence		Locality		F-Value
		Rural	Urban	
Low	Mean	109.23	109.37	14.45 **
	SD	6.75	6.01	
Moderate	Mean	127.47	128.76	
	SD	4.82	4.83	
High	Mean	143.43	144.95	
	SD	6.54	5.45	

**-Significant at 0.01 level

The above table clearly reveals that there is a significant mean difference between rural and urban intermediate students with reference to the levels of emotional intelligence. The mean values clearly indicates that there is the significant mean difference between urban rural students at low, moderate, high levels of emotional intelligence. Urban students are more emotionally intelligent than rural students at all levels.

Table 4.36: Levels of Emotional Intelligence based on Management

Levels of Emotional Intelligence		Management		F-Value
		Government	Private	
Low	Mean	109.55	110.19	9.81 **
	SD	6.87	5.86	
Moderate	Mean	127.48	128.73	
	SD	4.81	6.38	
High	Mean	143.51	145.17	
	SD	5.90	6.05	

**-Significant at 0.01 level

The table results clearly indicates that government and private college students are difference significance in their levels of emotional intelligence. The mean values shows that private college students are better than government college students with reference to their emotional intelligence at low, moderate and high levels.

HYPOTHESIS-19

There would be no significance difference in the levels of academic stress of intermediate students with respect to the variables gender, locality and type of management.

Table 4.37: Levels of Academic Stress based on Gender

Levels of Academic Stress		Gender		F-Value
		Male	Female	
Low	Mean	103.54	107.39	29.26**
	SD	8.49	7.69	
Moderate	Mean	123.05	125.37	
	SD	4.54	4.88	
High	Mean	143.55	141.24	
	SD	6.15	6.48	

**-Significant at 0.01 level

The obtained F value 29.26 table shows that there is a significant mean difference between boys and girls of intermediate course with reference to their levels of academic stress at low, moderate levels of academic stress. Girls are pruning to more academic stress than boys. At high levels of academic stress boys are exhibiting more academic stress than girls.

Table 4.38: Levels of Academic Stress based on Locality

Levels of Academic Stress		Locality		F-Value
		Rural	Urban	
Low	Mean	102.33	105.52	5.06 **
	SD	9.32	9.09	
Moderate	Mean	123.80	124.49	
	SD	4.67	5.89	
High	Mean	141.75	140.93	
	SD	6.97	6.01	

**-Significant at 0.01 level

The table values revels that the calculated value of F (5.06) is significant for urban and rural student's academic stress levels. The table mean values clearly reveals that urban students are having more academic stress than rural students at low and moderate level, in contrary, at high level of academic stress rural students are pruning to more academic stress than urban students.

Table 4.39: Levels of Academic Stress based on Management

Levels of Academic Stress		Management		F-Value
		Government	Private	
Low	Mean	104.80	105.01	7..86@
	SD	8.23	9.00	
Moderate	Mean	123.91	123.34	
	SD	6.15	5.85	
High	Mean	142.15	141.55	
	SD	6.46	6.79	

@-Not Significant

It can be seen from the above table results, that there is significant mean difference between government and private college students with reference to the levels of academic stress. The above table mean values shows that at low, moderate levels of academic stress private college students are more than the government students. At high level, the mean Academic stress scores of government college students are more than private college students. But the difference is significant and it concluded that at all levels academic stress of government and private college students is not similar.

FINDINGS OF THE STUDY

The major findings obtained through the analysis of the study are as follows.

1. There is significant influence of the main effects of gender, management and locality on emotional intelligence and academic stress of intermediate students.
2. There is significant impact of interaction effect of gender, management and locality on emotional intelligence and academic stress of intermediate students.
3. There is significant influence of Gender on Emotional Intelligence and Academic Stress of Intermediate Students.
4. There is significant influence of Management on Emotional Intelligence and Academic Stress of Intermediate Students.
5. There is no significant influence of Locality on Emotional Intelligence and Academic Stress of Intermediate Students.
6. There is significant influence of Nature of Course on Emotional Intelligence and Academic Stress of Intermediate Students.
7. There is significant influence of Medium of study on Emotional Intelligence and Academic Stress of Intermediate Students.
8. There is significant influence of Type of Residence on Emotional Intelligence and Academic Stress of Intermediate Students.
9. There is significant influence of Caste on Emotional Intelligence and Academic Stress of Intermediate Students.
10. There is significant influence of Father's Education on Emotional Intelligence and Academic Stress of Intermediate Students.
11. There is no significant influence of Mother's Education on Emotional Intelligence and Academic Stress of Intermediate Students.
12. There is significant influence of Father's Occupation on Emotional Intelligence and Academic Stress of Intermediate Students.
13. There is no significant influence of Mother's Occupation on Emotional Intelligence but Academic Stress is significantly influenced by Mothers occupation of Intermediate Students.
14. There is no significant influence of Family Income on Emotional Intelligence. There is a significant influence of family income on Academic Stress of Intermediate Students.
15. There is no significant influence of Size of the Family on Emotional Intelligence. There is a significant influence on size of family on Academic Stress of Intermediate Students.
16. There is significant influence of Type of the Family on Emotional Intelligence and Academic Stress of Intermediate Students.
17. These is a negative correlation between Emotional Intelligence and Academic Stress of Intermediate Students.

18. There is significant difference in the levels of Emotional Intelligence of Intermediate students with respect to the variables Gender, Locality and Type of management.
19. There is significant difference in the levels of Academic Stress of Intermediate students with respect to the variables Gender, Locality and Type of management.

Discussion of Findings of Study

Various studies on emotional intelligence and Academic stress among students are reviewed and reported on different types of variables. From the studies related to emotional intelligence with reference to the gender is observed that Saroj (2003), Suresh (2007), Ramana and Anithadevi (2018), Kumar (2020) found significant influence of gender on emotional intelligence. In the present investigation the researcher has attempted to find the significant mean difference between boys and girls studying Intermediate with regard to the Emotional Intelligence scores. Similarly from the studies related to Academic stress with reference to gender is also observed that Mishra and Manju (2018) Ravi (2018) Malammula (2020) found significant influence of gender on academic stress of students. In the present investigation the researcher made an attempt to find the mean difference between Boys and Girl students of Intermediate with reference to their Academic Stress scores.

Mahesh Harward (2015) Viquar Unnisa (2020) studied the influence of locality and type of management on Emotional Intelligence of students. In the present study, the researcher studied an influence of locality and type of management on Emotional intelligence and Academic Stress of Intermediate students. It is found significant mean difference between urban, rural and Government, Private college students with regard to their emotional intelligence and academic stress.

Makvana (2014) Balakishan Sharma (2011), Ramaprabhu, Dash (2018) conducted studies on Emotional Intelligence and Academic Stress with reference to achievement motivation of college students. They found that moderate Stress leads to high achievement motivation. The present study has enhanced the significance influence of course of study on Emotional Intelligence and academic stress of Intermediate students.

The above discussion reveals the significant influence of the variables gender, locality , management type of course on Emotional Intelligence and Academic stress of students.

CHAPTER 5

Summery and Conclusions

INTRODUCTION

This chapter deals with the summary of the study under the headings: Statement of the problem, need for the study, purpose of the study, scope of the study, objectives of the study, hypotheses of the study, variables included in the study, method of study, tools used, selection of sample, data collection, scoring and analysis, statistical techniques employed, major findings of the study, conclusions, educational implications and recommendations, limitations and suggestions for further research are investigated.

NEED AND SIGNIFICANCE OF STUDY

In today's highly competitive world, students face various academic problems including exam stress, disinterest in attending classes and inability to understand the subject. Academic stress is the feeling of anxiety or apprehension over one's performance in the academic activities. It can lead to students being unable to perform to the best of their abilities in examinations. At school/college there is a range of academic pressure feel, derived from a need for perfection, worry over grades, parental pressure, competition, sports, or a tough class load. The nervous breakdowns, panic attacks, burnouts, and depression are also apparent in many younger students. The same situation is not always stressful for all people, and all people do not undergo the same feelings or off-putting thoughts when stressed. Students were considered to be the future pillars who take the responsibilities to take our country to the next phase they should be in better way.

Students with high emotional quotient know and manage their own emotional life well and understand and deal effectively with the feelings of others. They are skillful in relationships. Intermediate course as an area of interdisciplinary knowledge is not merely an application of new core disciplines, but a praxis of a content where theories and practical wisdom are generated continuously. In working towards holistic approach to education, the importance of an emotionally supportive environment in the classroom is created by a teacher. Emotionally healthy behavior is reflected in characteristic ways of thinking, identifying, managing and expressing feelings and choosing effective behaviours. Emotional experience and expression are unique to each teacher and student. To know this, the investigator decided to analysis the emotional intelligence and academic stress among intermediate students.

STATEMENT OF THE PROBLEM

The present study is about Emotional Intelligence and „Academic stress of intermediate students with reference to various socio demographic variables. This study examines significant difference between selected variables among the selected sample of intermediate students in Andhra Pradesh. The present study is stated as *"Emotional Intelligence and Academic Stress of Higher Secondary Students"*.

OPERATIONAL DEFINITIONS

The operational definitions of the key terms are given below.

Emotional Intelligence: Emotional intelligence is the ability to monitor our own and other's felling and emotions, to discriminate among them, and to use this to guide our thinking and actions.

Academic Stress: Academic stress have included fear of falling behind with coursework, finding the motivation to study, time pressures, financial worries, and concern about academic ability.

Students: In the present study, the term students refer the 2nd year intermediate course.

Variable: Any trait that changes from one case or condition to another, more strictly the representation of the trait, usually in quantitative form, such as measurement or an enumeration.

Dependent variable: The dependent variable is one that the researcher is attempting to predict or explain. In the present study dependent variables are Emotional Intelligence and Academic Stress.

Independent variable: The variables that study the societal patterns and basic information about an individual. In this study Gender, Management, Locality, Nature of Course, Residence, Caste, Father's

Education, Mother's Education, Father's Occupation, Mother's Occupation, Annual Income of the Family, Size of the Family and Type of Family are considered as the Independent variables.

OBJECTIVES OF THE STUDY

Keeping in view of need of the study the following objectives are formulated for the present investigation.

1. To assess the level of emotional intelligence and academic stress among intermediate students.
2. To study the influence of main effect and interaction effect of gender, management and locality on emotional intelligence and academic stress among intermediate students.
3. To find weather there is any significant influence of the following Socio-Demographic variables on Emotional Intelligence and Academic Stress of Intermediate Students.
   - *(i)* Gender
   - *(ii)* Management
   - *(iii)* Locality
   - *(iv)* Nature of Course
   - *(v)* Medium
   - *(vi)* Caste
   - *(vii)* Father's Education
   - *(viii)* Mother's Education
   - *(ix)* Father's Occupation
   - *(x)* Mother's Occupation
   - *(xi)* Annual Income of the Family
   - *(xii)* Size of the Family
   - *(xiii)* Type of the Family
4. To find weather there is any significant relationship between emotional intelligence and academic stress of intermediate students.
5. To find the levels of Emotional Intelligence and Academic Stress of Intermediate students with reference to the main variables gender, locality and type of management.

HYPOTHESES OF THE STUDY

Based on the above objectives the following null hypotheses are formulated for the present study.

1. There would be no significant influence of the main effects of gender, management and locality on emotional intelligence and academic stress of intermediate students.

2. There would be no significant impact of interaction effect of gender, management and locality on emotional intelligence and academic stress of intermediate students.
3. There would be no significant influence of Gender on Emotional Intelligence and Academic Stress of Intermediate Students.
4. There would be no significant influence of Management on Emotional Intelligence and Academic Stress of Intermediate Students.
5. There would be no significant influence of Locality on Emotional Intelligence and Academic Stress of Intermediate Students.
6. There would be no significant influence of Nature of Course on Emotional Intelligence and Academic Stress of Intermediate Students.
7. There would be no significant influence of Medium on Emotional Intelligence and Academic Stress of Intermediate Students.
8. There would be no significant influence of Type of resience on Emotional Intelligence and Academic Stress of Intermediate Students.
9. There would be no significant influence of Caste on Emotional Intelligence and Academic Stress of Intermediate Students.
10. There would be no significant influence of Father's Education on Emotional Intelligence and Academic Stress of Intermediate Students.
11. There would be no significant influence of Mother's Education on Emotional Intelligence and Academic Stress of Intermediate Students.
12. There would be no significant influence of Father's Occupation on Emotional Intelligence and Academic Stress of Intermediate Students.
13. There would be no significant influence of Mother's Occupation on Emotional Intelligence and Academic Stress of Intermediate Students.
14. There would be no significant influence of Family Income on Emotional Intelligence and Academic Stress of Intermediate Students.
15. There would be no significant influence of Size of the Family on Emotional Intelligence and Academic Stress of Intermediate Students.
16. There would be no significant influence of Type of the Family on Emotional Intelligence and Academic Stress of Intermediate Students.

17. These would be no significant relationship between Emotional Intelligence and Academic Stress of Intermediate Students.
18. There would be no significant difference in the levels of Emotional Intelligence of Intermediate students with respect to the variables Gender, Locality and Type of management.
19. There would be no significant difference in the levels of Academic Stress of Intermediate students with respect to the variables Gender, Locality and Type of management.

SCOPE OF THE STUDY

The intention of the study is to make a survey of emotional intelligence and academic stress of different methods of studying of intermediate course located in Gutur, Prakasam and Nellore districts of Andhra Pradesh state constituted the population of the study. The study attempted to identify the influence between the dependent variables are Emotional Intelligence & Academic Stress and the independent variables like Gender, Management, Locality, Nature of Course, Medium, Religion, Caste, Father's Education, Mother's Education, Father's Occupation, Mother's Occupation, Annual Income of the Family, Size of the Family and Type of the Family.

REVIEW OF RELATED LITERATURE

In the review of related literature, there are studies which shows the influence of various socio demographic variables on emotional Intelligence and Academic Stress.

Mishra and Manju (2018) Saleh Alsulami (2008) studied the academic stress levels of the students and the significant influence of gender. Ramana and Anitha Devi 2018 Kumar 2020 conducted studies on Emotional Intelligence of students. Various studies have been conducted on Emotional Intelligence and Academic stress of students with reference to gender, locality and Type of management etc... very few studies are conducted with reference to the variables type of family, income of family father's occupation and Mother's occupation. In order to fill the research gap the investigator felt the need to study the influence of specific variables on Emotional intelligence and Academic stress of students at intermediate level.

VARIABLES OF THE STUDY

In this study the following variables were taken in to consideration.

A. Dependent variables:

(a) Emotional Intelligence
(b) Academic Stress

B. Independent variables

I. Socio-Demographic variables

(i) Gender
(ii) Management
(iii) Locality
(iv) Nature of Course
(v) Medium
(vi) Caste
(vii) Father's Education
(viii) Mother's Education
(ix) Father's Occupation
(x) Mother's Occupation
(xi) Annual Income of the Family
(xii) Size of the Family
(xiii) Type of the Family

DESIGN OF THE STUDY

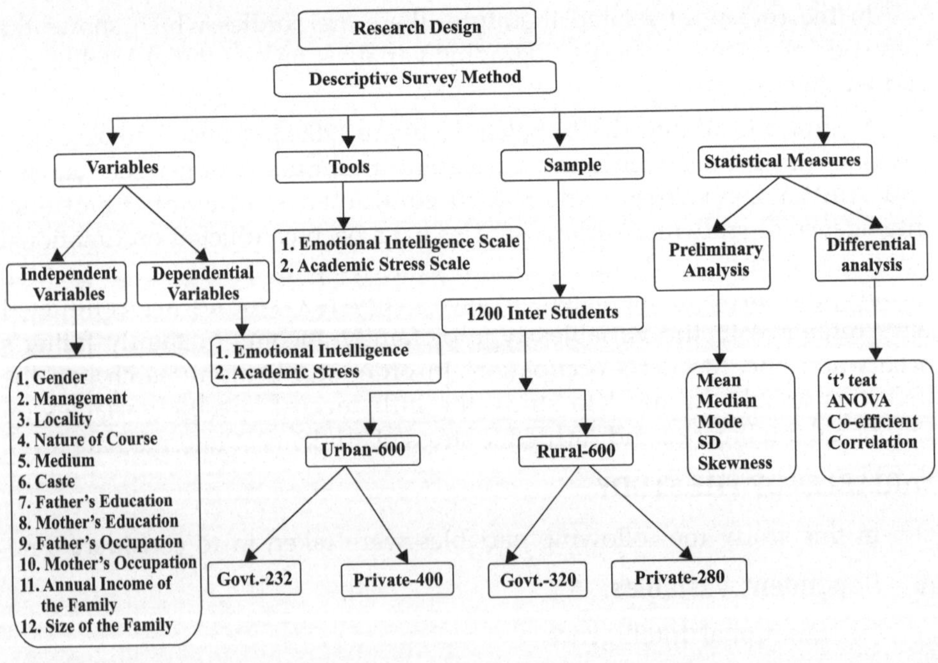

TOOLS USED FOR THE STUDY

Tools used for the purpose of data collection in the present study are:

1. **Emotional Intelligence Scale:** The Emotional Intelligence of the Subjects was assessed by using Emotional Intelligence Scale developed by Nutankumar Thingujam, and Usha Ram (1999). It consists of 33 items. Each question has 5-Options. The Items are scored with the help of Scoring key. The reliability of the instrument 0.90 was established by test-retest method and the validity is 0.78.

   The test Emotional intelligence scale was scored by giving weightages to the responses 5, 4, 3, 2 and 1. The maximum score 165 and minimum score 33 obtained by adding the weightages on all these items. Appropriate coding is given to the response given to personal variables.

2. **Assessment of Students Academic Stress Scale:** Students Academic Stress Scale was developed and standardized by Kumar Reddy B.S (1999). It consisted of 40 items and sub divided into five components having eight items in each category. 1. Personal inadequacy (F1), 2. Fear of failure (F2), Interpersonal difficulties with teachers (F3), 4.Teacher /pupil relationship/teaching methods (F4) and 5. Inadequate study facilities (F5).

   Students Academic Stress scale was score by giving weightages to the responses 0-1-2-3 and 4. The Maximum score 160 and Minimum score 40 obtained by adding the weightages on all these items.

3. **Personal data sheet:** Personal data sheet was developed by the investigator to measure the impact of socio demographic variables on Emotional Intelligence and Academic Stress among intermediate students.

SAMPLE OF THE STUDY

Intermediate students studying in Guntur, Prakasam and Nellore districts of Andhra Pradesh state constituted the population of the study. There are 1900 girls students and 1200 boys students. So, the total population of 3100 Intermediate students constituted the study.

Among 3100 Intermediate students 1200 students are selected randomly as sample of the study. Four government and private colleges located in urban and rural areas of the each of the above districts were selected randomly. After selection of the colleges, 2nd year intermediate students from Arts and Science groups of these colleges are selected randomly.

PROCEDURE OF DATA COLLECTION

The investigator personally visited the intermediate colleges and the principals were requested to permit the researcher for collection of data in their institutions. The program and the time schedule were communicated to all the staff of concerned lecturers of the colleges in advance and obtained permission from them.

In each college, the required number of intermediate 2nd year students from different courses i.e., H.E.C, C.E.C, M.P.C, Bi.P.C, M.E.C and H.T.C have been selected using systematic random sampling method. The students were well motivated before attempting the tests.

The test booklets and answer sheets were distributed among the selected students. The instructions were read out and the purpose of investigation was explained to motivate them to give answers in a proper manner. Sufficient time was provided for the students to give answers to all the questions in questionnaires. The investigator took care to ensure that all questions were answered by the students following instructions.

Emotional intelligence scale and socio demographic sheet were distributed in the morning session one after the other with a break of 10 minutes. After providing sufficient time the investigator has collected the booklets and answer sheets.

In the afternoon students academic stress scale was distributed to the same group of students. Students were instructed on how to answer the academic stress scale. They were assured that the information given by them would be kept confidential.

The investigator requested the students to respond to the questions genuinely. After successful completion of the test, the investigator collected the booklets and answer sheets.

ANALYSIS OF DATA

On the basis of the hypotheses of the investigation, statistical analysis is carried out by employing appropriate statistical techniques. Frequency distribution tables are prepared for emotional intelligence and academic stress scores for whole group. Mean, Median. Mode, Range, Quartile Deviation, Standard Deviation, Skewness, Kurtosis, Coefficient of correlation were calculated wherever necessary. The significance tests like t test and F test were employed. All the above calculations were done by using the SPSS software.

FINDINGS OF THE STUDY

1. There is significant influence of the main effects of gender, management and locality on emotional intelligence and academic stress of intermediate students.
2. There is significant impact of interaction effect of gender, management and locality on emotional intelligence and academic stress of intermediate students.

3. There is significant influence of Gender on Emotional Intelligence and Academic Stress of Intermediate Students.
4. There is significant influence of Management on Emotional Intelligence and Academic Stress of Intermediate Students.
5. There is no significant influence of Locality on Emotional Intelligence and Academic Stress of Intermediate Students.
6. There is significant influence of Nature of Course on Emotional Intelligence and Academic Stress of Intermediate Students.
7. There is significant influence of Medium of study on Emotional Intelligence and Academic Stress of Intermediate Students.
8. There is significant influence of Type of Residence on Emotional Intelligence and Academic Stress of Intermediate Students.
9. There is significant influence of Caste on Emotional Intelligence and Academic Stress of Intermediate Students.
10. There is significant influence of Father's Education on Emotional Intelligence and Academic Stress of Intermediate Students.
11. There is no significant influence of Mother's Education on Emotional Intelligence and Academic Stress of Intermediate Students.
12. There is significant influence of Father's Occupation on Emotional Intelligence and Academic Stress of Intermediate Students.
13. There is no significant influence of Mother's Occupation on Emotional Intelligence but Academic Stress is significantly influenced by Mothers occupation of Intermediate Students.
14. There is no significant influence of Family Income on Emotional Intelligence.

    There is a significant influence of family income on Academic Stress of Intermediate Students.
15. There is no significant influence of Size of the Family on Emotional Intelligence.

    There is a significant influence on size of family on Academic Stress of Intermediate Students.
16. There is significant influence of Type of the Family on Emotional Intelligence and Academic Stress of Intermediate Students.
17. These is a negative correlation between Emotional Intelligence and Academic Stress of Intermediate Students.
18. There is significant difference in the levels of Emotional Intelligence of Intermediate students with respect to the variables Gender, Locality and Type of management.
19. There is significant difference in the levels of Academic Stress of Intermediate students with respect to the variables Gender, Locality and Type of management.

EDUCATIONAL IMPLICATIONS AND RECOMMENDATIONS

In the present study, on the basis of the results the following educational implications are made.

- Students should learn to deal with their expanding social universe and necessarily attain certain degree of emotional intelligence to ward of deviances.
- Teachers should express their concern towards students by spending more time to interact with them, to make them feel free to exchange their ideas and feelings which in turn enhance their emotional intelligence as well as academic achievement.
- Teachers should observe college environment, study habits/skills and motivation of adolescents in order to reduce their academic stress.
- Students with high emotional intelligence can with stand the academic stress and still are able to better in their academic achievement.
- A student who has high emotional intelligence can be psychologically healthy, so that he can face any hurdle that comes in his academic life and perform better.
- High emotional intelligence among intermediate students will also enhance their problem-solving ability.

LIMITATIONS OF THE STUDY AND SUGGESTIONS FOR FURTHER RESEARCH

The following limitations are observed in this investigation

- The present study is confined to 1200 intermediate students only. It is suggested that future researchers may under take studies with larger sample.
- The effect of only a few independent variables on emotional intelligence and academic stress has been studied.
- The study is confined to intermediate course only.
- A similar investigation may try conducted by taking students from different classes also namely VIII, IX and X classes, graduation, post graduate courses and professional courses.
- The study is confined only to the intermediate students of the government and Private colleges.
- Only very few socio-demographic variables and psycho-sociological variables are studied in the present study. Some other variables like merits, attendance, and regularity of students etc. may help to know their impact on emotional intelligence and academic stress.

- The study indicates that academic stress has originated from personal inadequacy, fear of failure, interpersonal difficulties, poor teacher-pupil relations, and inadequate study facilities. If these problems are unchecked at an early stage, they may have damaging effects at later years. Thus, the findings of the study point an urgent need to develop interventions and implement programmes to reduce academic stress of intermediate students.
- Research in this area is yet to receive its due recognition as a special area. The present status as far as the Indian educational and psychological research is concerned, in its first phase, requires conducting national wide surveys to study the tenth class students with academic stresses. This would help us to know more about the sources of stresses. It would also lead us finding a ways to get rid of the two main ailments viz. Stagnations and waste. Identification of students with academic stress would necessitate the development of remedial program in the next phase.
- Psychologists, teachers and counselors should take initiative steps to promote academic achievement of the students of private schools by assessing the student, delivering assessments with care, maximizing learning choices, remedial programmes. The counselors also need to extend their expertise in developing behavior modification techniques and intervention programmes to improve the academic achievement of the students of government schools.
- Steps initiated towards this end would ultimately result in alleviating the problems of students and improving their high level of emotional intelligence.

CONCLUSION

It has been an exciting experience for the investigator in undertaking the research on emotional intelligence and academic stress among intermediate students. The major purpose of this study was to examine relationship between emotional intelligence and academic stress. Depending on the findings of the study, the following concluding notes were made: There is a significant relationship between emotional intelligence and academic stress. There is a significant difference in emotional intelligence among undergraduate students with respect to their gender, male students have higher emotional intelligence compared to female students. There is significant difference in academic stress among intermediate students with respect to their gender , medium of instruction, course of study etc. There is need to develop more and more action on account of develops high emotional intelligence and reducing academic stress. Thus the present investigation becomes a humble contribution in this direction. In addition, it has revealed the relative importance of emotional intelligence and academic stress of intermediate students. Further, it has brought out the need for providing a variety of activities and programmes for students in order to develop better academic achievement among intermediate students that are stressed in NEP-2019 also in Kothari Commission report.

Bibliography

Abdul Rahman Al Asmari (2014). Emotional Intelligence and Academic Achievement: A Comparative, Gender-Based Study of Undergraduate English Language Learners in Saudi Arabia. Journal of Education and Practice, 5(6), 12-19.

Abiodun Musbau Lawal, Erhabor Sunday Idemudia & Tema Senyatsi (2018). Emotional Intelligence and Mental Health: An Exploratory Study with South African University Students, Journal of Psychology in Africa, 28(6), 492-497.

Abouserie, R. (1994). Sources and Levels of Stress in Relation to Locus of Control and Self-esteem in University Students. *Educational Psychology,* 14, 323-330.

Ali Khanehkeshi and Basavarajappa (2012). The Relationship of Academic Stress with Aggression, Depression and Academic Performance of College Students in Iran. *Journal on Educational Psychology,* 5(1), 24-31.

Amirtha, M. Kadhiravan, S. (2006); Influence of Personality on the Emotional Intelligence of Teachers. *EDUTRACKS – August.*

Anbumalar C., Dorathy Agines P., Jaswanti V.P., Priya and D. Reniangelin D. (2017). Gender Differences in Perceived Stress Levels and Coping Strategies among College Students. The International Journal of Indian Psychology, 4(4), 23-33.

Atilgan Erözkan (2013). Exploring the Relationship between Perceived Emotional Intelligence and Coping Skills of Undergraduate Students. International Journal of Human Sciences. 10(1), 1537-1549.

Bala, M. Agarwal, R. Sarna. R.P. (2009). Studied the Gender differences as Associated with Mental Health of the College going Students of Various Faculties, Behavioral Scientist, 10(2), pp.119-126.

Balkishan Sharma, Rajshekhar Wavare, Ajit Deshpande, Richa Nigam and Ramkrishna Chandorkar (2011). A Study of Academic Stress and its Effect on Vital Parameters in Final Year Medical Students at SAIMS Medical College, Indore, Madhya Pradesh. *Biomedical Research, 22* (3), Pp: 361-365.

Bang, E. (2009). The Effects of Gender, Academic Concerns, and Social Support on Stress for International Students.

Bar-On, R. (1997). Emotional Intelligence Quotient Inventory. Toronto, D.N. Multi-Health Systems, Inc.

Bharadwaj, R. (1997) A Study of N-achievement in Relation to Adequate Expression and Control of Emotion and Sex among Handicapped and Non-handicapped. *Indian Journal of Psychology,* 72(1 and 2); 53-58.

Bharadwaj, R.L. (1998); Emotional Competencies as Associated with Early Adolescent Labors and Non-labors of both Sexes *Indian Journal of Psychology,* 73(1and 2); 3-8.

Bhavin U Pandya, Revati C Deshpande and Anushree Karani (2012). A Study on Impact of Academic Stress on MBA Students of Gujarat Technological University. *International Refereed Research Journal,* III, 3(3), Pp: 20-28.

Bhupinder Pal Singh (2011). Study and Analysis of Academic Stress of B.Ed. Students. *International Journal of Educational Planning & Administration,*1(2), Pp: 119-127.

Bibi et al., (2016). Relationship between Emotional Intelligence and Self Esteem among Pakistani University Students. Cell & Developmental Biology, 6(4).

Bindu and Immanuel (2006). Gender Differences in Emotional Intelligence, Psychological Studies 51(4): 261-268.

Boludola G. Owolabi (2013). Impact of Emotional Intelligence Training on Academic Stress among Secondary School Students in Ibadan. *Journal of Capital Development in Behavioural Sciences.*

Brinda Sharma (2013). Family Relationship Pattern and Mental Health in Adolescents. International Journal of Advancements in Research & Technology, 2(2), 1-8.

Chandan and Shivappa (2020). Academic Stress among Higher Secondary School Students: an Overview. Semantic Scholar, 1(2), 25-34.

Charanjeev Singh, Sunita Sharma and Ravinder Kumar Sharma (2011). Level of Stress and Coping Strategies used by Nursing Interns. *Nursing and Midwifery Research Journal,* 7(4), Pp: 152-160.

Ciarrochi, J., Chan, A. & Bagar, J. (2002) Measuring Emotional Intelligence in Adolescents. *Journal of Personality and Individual difference. 31(7)*

Deepa Ghosh (2015). Gender Differences in Emotional Intelligence and Self Concept of the Tribal and Non-Tribal Higher School Students. International Journal of Social Sciences Review, 3(1), 1-7.

Dewan (2003). Effect of Stress, Locality and Gender on selected Cognitive and Non-cognitive Variables.*Unpublished Ph.D., Thesis, Panjab University, Chandigarh.*

Dharvinder Singh et al., (2016). Emotional Intelligencein Relation to Academic Achievement of Secondary School Students. Shrinkhla Ek Shodhparak Vaicharik Patrika, 3(3), 71-73.

Elzubeir, Elzubeir and Magzoub (2010). Stress and Coping Strategies among Arab Medical Students: Towards a Research Agenda. Edu Health, 233-235.

Fathima and Neelakandan (2011) Tried to Identify the Human well-being through Emotional Intelligence among the College going Students. Journal of Psycho Social Research, 6 (1).

Fida, Asfandyar; Ghaffar, Abdul; Zaman, Amir; Satti, Asif Niwaz (2018). Gender Comparison of Emotional Intelligence of University Students, *Journal of Education and Educational Development*, 5(1), 172-188.

Garima Gupta and Sushil Kumar (2010). Mental Health in Relation to Emotional Intelligence and Self Efficacy among College Students, Journal of the Indian Academy of Applied Psychology, Vol. 36, No. 1, 61-67.

Goleman, D. (1995). Emotional Intelligence: Why it can matter more than IQ. New York: Bantom Books.

Hamilton. S and Fagot. BI. (1988). Chronic Stress and Coping Styles: A Comparison of Male and Female Undergraduates. *J PersSoc Psychol.* 55(5), Pp: 819-823.

Huan, Yeo, Ang, and Chong (2005). The Influence of Dispositional Optimism and Gender on Adolescents' Perception of Academic Stress. Adolescence Fall, 41(163), 533-46.

Huey-Fen Wang [1], Mei Chang Yeh (1992). Stress, Coping, and Psychological Health of Vocational High School Nursing Students Associated with a Competitive Entrance Exam. J Nurs Res, 13(2), 106-16.

Hussain, A., Kumar, A., & Husain, A. (2008). Academic Stress and Adjustment among High School Students. Journal of the Indian Academy of Applied Psychology, 34, 70-73.

Jane Waithira Karimi, Jacinta Aswani Kwena & Alice Anika (2020). Emotional Intelligence and Academic Achievement among Secondary School Students in Kilifi County, Kenya: A Correlational Study. JRIIE, 4(2), 32-42.

Jayasankara Reddy, Karishmarajanmenon and Anjanathattil (2018). Academic Stress and its Sources Among University Students. Biomed Pharmacol J, 11(1).

Jones MC, Johnston. DW. (1997). Distress, Stress and Coping in First-year Student Nurses. *PubMed,* 26(3), Pp: 475-82.

Jose. A. Piqueras (2011). Relationship between Emotional Intelligence and Stress Coping Strategies. *Acadimiaedu.*, 37, Pp: 1-24.

Katyal, Sudha, Vasudeva and Pramila (2001). Effects of Socio-personal Factors in Academic Stress among Adolescents. Indian J. Appl. Psychol., 35: 35-37.

Kavitha, A (2011) *A Comparative Study to Assess the Growth and Development of Toddlers in Rural and Urban Areas.* Master's Thesis, Dr. G. Sakunthala College of Nursing, Trichy.

Kiran Pal Singh Chawla and Archana Agrawal (2021). Academic Stress on Higher Secondary Students: A Review. *International Journal of Multidisciplinary,* 6(1): 79-83.

Laigong Beatrice Chemutai and Shikuku M. Mulambula (2020). The Determination of Academic Stress Levels by Gender and Year of Study. A Case of Kenyan University Students. *American International Journal of Social Science,* 9(4), 16-22.

Lauren A. Gentry, Jane J. Chung, Nandar Aung, Stefan Keller, Katie M. Heinrich, and Jay E. Maddock (2007). Gender Differences in Stress and Coping among Adults living in Hawai.*L. A. Gentry et al./Californian Journal of Health Promotion,* 5(2), Pp: 89-102.

Mahesh Bharvad (2015). A Study of Emotional Intelligence and Adjustment among School Students. International Journal of Indian Psychology, 2 (2), 25-30.

Mahmood Ahmad Khan and Mohammad Muzzafar Lone (2015). Emotional Intelligence of Rural and Urban Post Graduate Students of Kashmir University. Periodic Research, 3(4), 180-184.

Mahmood Ahmad Khan and Nisar Ahmad Bhat (2013). Emotional Intelligence of Adolescent Boys and Girls. International Journal of Educational Research and Development, 2(3), 67-71.

Mannapur B. et al (2010). A Study of Psychological Stress in Undergraduate Medical Students at S N Medical College, Bagalkot, Karnataka. *Journal of Clinical and Diagnostic Research.* 4(4), Pp: 2869-2874.

Mayer, J.D., & Salovey, P. (1995); Emotional Intelligence and the Construction and Regulation of Feelings. Applied & Preventive Psychology, 4(3); 197-208.

Mayor, J.D.; Salovey, P. & Caruso, D. (2000). Models of Emotional Intelligence. In R. Sternberg. Hand Book of Intelligence. Cambridge. U.K. Cambridge University Press.

Mishra and Manju (2018). A Comparative Study on Academic Stress Level of Male and Female B.Ed. Students. Indian Journal of Health and Wellbeing, 9(1), 131-135.

Misra, R. & McKean, M. (2000). College Students Academic Stress and its Relation to their Anxiety, Time Management and Leisure Satisfaction. *American Journal of Health Studies*,16 (1): 41-50.

Nuthan Kumar. S. Thingujam (2002) Emotional Intelligence: What is the evidence? *Journal of Psychological studies. Vol. 47; No (1-3).*

Nuthan Kumar. S. Thingujam (2002) Emotional Intelligence: What is the evidence? Journal of Psychological Studies. 47(1-3).

Pathan (2004). Emotional Intelligence of Secondary Teachers at D.Ed. College, Navapur, Maharashtra. Cited in University News.

Patil, B. and Kumar, A. (2006). Emotional Intelligence among Student Teachers in Relation to Sex, Faculty and Academic Achievement. Indian Educational Abstracts, 6(2), p. 56.

Pau., A K H, Croucher, R., Sohanpal, R., Muirhead, V., and K Seymour (2004). To Explore how Dental Undergraduates with different Levels of Emotional Intelligence (EI) Cope with Stress. *British Dental Journal*, 197 (4), Pp: 167-221.

Petrides, K.V. & Furnham, A. (2000). Gender differences in measured and self-estimated Trait Emotional Intelligence. Sex Roles, 42(5), 449-461.

Prabu Suresh P (2015). A Study on Academic Stress among Higher Secondary Stress, *International Journal of Humanities and Social Science Invention*, 4(10), 63-68.

Pradhan et al., (1999). Employee Performance at Workplace: Conceptual Model and Empirical Validation. Business Perspectives and Research, 5(1), 69-85.

Rajendran, R., & Kaliappan, K.V. (1990). Efficacy of Behavioural Programme in Managing the Academic Stress and Improving Academic Performance. *Journal of Personality and Clinical Studies*, 6(2), 193-196.

Rakesh Bharti (2013). The Effect of Emotional Intelligence on Achievement Stress of Student-Teachers. PARIPEX - Indian Journal of Research. 2(8), 91-93.

Ramana K.1, S. Anitha Devi (2018). The Relationship between Emotional Intelligence and Academic Achievement among Intermediate Students, IOSR Journal of Business and Management (IOSRJBM), 20, (4), 30-35.

Ramaprabou, Dash and Sasi Kanta (2018). Effect of Academic Stress on Achievement Motivation among College Students. i-manager's Journal on Educational Psychology, 11(4), 32-34.

Ramesh Singh Bartwal and Anoj Raj (2013). Academic Stress among School going Adolescents in Relation to their Emotional Intelligence. *International Journal of Innovative Research & Development*, 2(11), Pp: 416-424.

Ranjitha and Michelle (2000). College Students' Academic Stress and its Relation to their Anxiety, Time Management, and Leisure Satisfaction. American Journal of Health Studies, 16, 41-51.

Ravi Sadda (2018). Effect of Academic Stress on Intermediate Students-A Study. *American International Journal of Research in Humanities, Arts and Social Sciences*, 55-58.

Razia. B. (2016). Academic Stress of Adolescents in Government and Private Schools. International Journal of Scientific Research, 5(1), 414-416.

Robert J Murphy, Sarah A Gray, Gerald Sterling, Kathleen Reeves and Joseph DuCette (2009). A Comparative Study of Professional Student Stress. J Dent Educ, 73(3), 328-337.

Ruth Lo (2002). A Longitudinal Study of Perceived Level of Stress, Coping and Self-esteem of Undergraduate Nursing Students: An Australian Case Study. JAN Leading Global Research, 39(2), 119-126.

S.M. Makvana. (2014). Emotional Intelligence as A Related to Difference Areas, Stream' And Sex' Among School Student. International Journal of Indian Psychology. 1(2), 1-9.

Sahana Madhyastha, Latha and Asha Kamath (2014). Stress and Coping among Final year Medical Students. *AP J Psychol Med*, 15 (1), Pp: 74-80.

Saleh Alsulami, Zaid Al Omar, Mohammed S Binnwejim, Fahad Alhamdan, Amr Aldrees, Abdulkarim Al-Bawardi, Meshary Alsohim and Mohammed Alhabeeb (2018). Perception of Academic Stress among Health Science Preparatory Program Students in Two Saudi Universities. Adv Med Educ Pract, 12(9), 159-164.

Salovey, P. and Mayor, D.D. (1990). Emotional Intelligence, Imagination. Cognition and Personality, 9(3), 185-211.

Salovey, P., Bedell, B.T., Detweiler, J.B., & Mayer, J.D. (2000). Current Directions in Emotional Intelligence Research. *Handbook of Emotions New York: Guilford Press*. Pp: 504-520.

Sanjeev Kumar and J.P. Bhukar (2013). The Aim of this Study was to Investigate the Stress Levels and Coping Strategies of Professional Students belonging to Physical Education and Engineering Professions. *Journal of Physical Education and Sports Management*, 4(1), 5-11.

Seyedeh Najmeh Noorbakhsha, Mohammad Ali Besharata and Jamileh Zareia (2010). Emotional Intelligence and Coping Styles with Stress. Procedia Social and Behavioral Sciences, 5, 818-822.

Shycil Mathew (2017). A Comparative Study on Academic Stress and Coping Strategies between Adolescents Studying in Selected Urban and Rural Colleges at Mangalore. International Journal of Comprehensive and Advanced Pharmacology, October-December, 2(4),124-130.

Singh, A., and Upadhyay, A. 2008. Age and Sex Differences in Academic Stress among College Students. Social Science International, 24(1), 78-88.

Singh. A and Singh. S., (2008). Stress and Adjustment among Professional and Non-professional Students. *Industrial Psychiatry Journal.* 17 (1), 26-27.

Snehlata D. Ghatol (2017). Academic Stress among Higher Secondary School Students: A Review. International Journal of Advanced Research in Education & Technology, 4(1), 38-41.

Subramani, C. and Kadhiravan, S. (2017). Academic Stress and Mental Health among High School Students. *Indian Journal of Applied Research,* 7(5).

Sukhpal Kaur, Karobi Das, Amrinder, Neha, Kanika, Sukhjit, Meena, Pooja, Gagandeep, Isha, Arash, Rajina (2009). That Stress and Coping in the Nursing Students. *Journal of Mental Health & Human Behavior,* 2, (6), Pp: 51-56.

Supe. A.N., (2010). A Study of Stress in Medical Students at Seth G.S. Medical College. *Journal of Post Graduate Medicine,* 44 (1*): 1-6.*

Suvarna, V. D. (2014). The Present Study is concerned with the Stress Management and Emotional Intelligence of 378 Students Studying B Ed in Mandya District. *International Multidisciplinary Research Journal,* 2(6), Pp: 1-5.

Throndike E.L. (1920). Intelligence and its uses Harperls Magazine, 140, 227-235.

Umar, Usman Sani (2019). Impact of Academic Stress and Coping Strategies among Senior Secondary School Students in Kaduna State, Nigeria. *International Journal of Innovative Social & Science Education Research,* 7(1): 40-44.

Usha and Rekha (2009). Emotional Competence and Mental Health as Predictors of Academic Achievement. Edutrack, 8(10): 25-29.

Venkateswar Meher, Rajashree Baral and Sadhujan Bankira (2021). An Analysis of Emotional Intelligence and Academic Performance of Four - Year Integrated B.Ed. Trainees Sadhujan Bankira. Shanlax International Journal of Education 9(2): 108-116.

Viquar Unnisa (2020). A Study of Emotional Intelligence among Secondary School Students. Aegaeum Journal, 8(8), 1275-1283.

Zeynep Kalyoncu, Semra Guney, MahmutArslan, Salih Guney and Evren Ayranci (2012). Analysis of the Relationship between Emotional Intelligence and Stress caused by the Organisation: A Study of Nurses. Business Intelligence Journal, 5(2), Pp: 334-346.

Index

❑ ❑ ❑ ❑ ❑